Best Sussex Walks

David Bathurst

summersdale

Summersdale Publishers Ltd
46 West Street
Chichester
West Sussex
PO19 1RP
UK

www.summersdale.com

Printed and bound in Great Britain.

ISBN: 1 84024 3406

Line drawing by Terry Whitlock
Maps by Bill Le Bihan
www.oldbill.demon.co.uk

Acknowledgements

I wish to acknowledge the help and support of a number of people in putting this book together: Rachael Osborne and all her colleagues at Summersdale Publishers for their enthusiasm, efficiency and support; Bill Le Bihan who has provided the magnificent maps to accompany the text; Terry Whitlock for his delightful illustration for the book; my wife Susan for her constant love, support and patience; and lastly my little daughter Jennifer Rose who, as an involuntary but uncomplaining travelling companion during the planning stages, must know some of these walks quite well herself now!

About the Author

David Bathurst was born in Guildford in 1959 and has enjoyed writing and walking throughout his adult life. He has walked all the principal long-distance paths in Great Britain, and his guide to walking these routes, entitled *The Beaten Track*, was published by Summersdale in 2001. He has written nine other books, including a guide to walking the coastline of Sussex which appeared in 2002, as well as books on children's literature and the work of magistrates' courts.

David's chief claim to fame is his recitation of all four Gospels from memory in a single day in 1998, and he recited the Book of Psalms, the longest book of the Bible, from memory in one day in 2002. By profession he is a legal adviser to the magistrates sitting at Chichester and Worthing.

He lives in Barnham in West Sussex with his wife Susan and daughter Jennifer Rose.

Contents

Introduction 7

Chapter One: Best Railway Walk...................................13

Chapter Two: Best Town Walk 23

Chapter Three: Best Village Walk 35

Chapter Four: Best Woodland Walk 47

Chapter Five: Best Heritage Walk 60

Chapter Six: Best Literary Walk 68

Chapter Seven: Best Ghost Walk 82

Chapter Eight: Best Pub Walk 94

Chapter Nine: Best Sunday Afternoon Walk ...D+J 06....108

Chapter Ten: Best Church Walk 116

Chapter Eleven: Best Hilltop Walk 132

Chapter Twelve: Best Waterside Walk 143

Chapter Thirteen: Best Family Walk 158

Chapter Fourteen: Best Nature Lover's Walk 167

Chapter Fifteen: Best Coastal Walk 180

Chapter Sixteen: Best Teashop Walk ..D.f.J..0.9.......193

Chapter Seventeen: Best Challenge Walk 206

Introduction

It is not surprising that, with so much splendid walking available in Sussex, there should be a wealth of books describing walks in the county. However, I am unaware of any book that offers the best *themed* walks in the county. This book aims to fill that gap, providing what I consider to be the best walk in Sussex in seventeen different categories: Waterside, Family, Teashop, Challenge, Pub, Sunday Afternoon, Hilltop, Church, Town, Village, Railway, Ghost, Woodland, Nature Lover's, Literary, Coastal and Heritage.

Naturally, it is not possible to be completely objective about what makes the best walk in the categories given, and some readers may disagree with my choices. My selection is based on a number of factors. Firstly, I have endeavoured to aim for parity of walking between East and West Sussex (eight of the walks are in East Sussex, nine are in West Sussex). Secondly, I have tried to avoid any overlap between walks; the only overlap that exists is a very small section of the Teashop and Challenge walks. Thirdly, I have purposely started and finished each walk at a place that is well served by public transport as well as by road. Fourthly, I have tried to include a number of walks which can be managed by those of limited physical capability, including pushchair and wheelchair users. The walks in this book cover a range of distances between two and thirty miles, with some capable of being completed within an hour, and others requiring a full day at the very least.

Fifthly, I have ensured that all the walks use existing public rights of way. Finally, I have tried to cover all the significant visitor attractions in East and West Sussex, including the cities of Chichester and Brighton; the towns of Rye, Midhurst, Petworth, Arundel, Steyning, Lewes, Eastbourne, Hastings and Battle; the villages of Bosham, Amberley, Findon,

Alfriston, Wilmington, Hartfield and Winchelsea; areas of great natural beauty including Chichester Harbour, the South Downs, the Seven Sisters, Ashdown Forest, Kingley Vale Nature Reserve and Hastings Country Park; and classic beauty spots including Harting Down, Chanctonbury Ring, Cissbury Ring and Beachy Head. By the time you've completed all the walks in this book, you should be an expert on the history, countryside and wildlife of Sussex – not to mention its pubs and teashops.

There truly is something for everybody in Sussex. The book-lover can be immersed in the myriad literary associations of Rye; the church historian will, on a day's walk in West Sussex, meet a vast range of ecclesiastical architecture from a lofty college chapel to a cosy country church with ancient wallpaintings; the walker in search of unspoilt downland countryside and majestic views will love the hilltop march from Amberley to Findon; and even those with an interest in the paranormal are not neglected, as an innocuous walk through the streets of Brighton conjures up memories of ghostly apparitions of bygone years.

Each walk described in this book is accompanied by a map and prefaced by essential information including accessibility by car and public transport, length, duration, refreshment facilities en route, and conditions. This information should indicate to you whether you are capable of completing the walk, given the physical fitness of you and your walking companions, and the time of year you are thinking of undertaking the walk. If you're not sure whether you are capable of completing a given walk, the simple answer is to go on some practice walks round your locality and these will tell you how many miles you can reasonably manage, although bear in mind that several walks in this book do require some up-and-down work.

Which brings me to the subject of equipment. None of

the walks in the book require specialist walking or climbing equipment – the terrain is never severe enough for that – but there are some minimum requirements which apply to virtually all the walks. What you wear, and what you take with you, will of course depend on the nature of the walk and the weather conditions. If, for instance, you are doing the Best Teashop Walk on a pleasant summer's day, you could comfortably complete it in ordinary day clothes and comfortable shoes, and with no equipment other than this book and perhaps a newspaper to read while waiting for your tea. However, if you are tackling the Best Hilltop Walk on a very cold winter's day – and a crisp clear sunny day in winter makes this walk especially rewarding – you will need a pair of high-quality walking shoes or boots, warm clothing, a thermos of hot tea or coffee, and ideally some nourishing food as there are no en-route refreshment opportunities. Any walk that takes you outside a city or town will require comfortable and stout footwear, waterproofs if it is raining or likely to rain, and some refreshment both of the solid and liquid (non-alcoholic!) variety. If you are walking in hot weather, you will need to drink plenty of water. Don't wait until you are thirsty before you do. The Best Challenge Walk brings its own special logistical problems which are detailed in the chapter devoted to that walk. And if you will forgive me for saying it, always have a good breakfast before you set out!

It should go without saying that you must have the utmost respect and courtesy for the countryside, observing the Country Code and avoiding doing anything which spoils the surroundings or puts yourself, other people or animals at risk. Be particularly careful about straying too close to cliff edges, and *never* allow yourself to be put in danger of being cut off by an incoming tide. None of the walking is so remote from civilisation that you are likely to be stranded or benighted for any reason, but it makes sense to avoid setting out into the countryside in particularly adverse weather conditions. If you do, you should have a mobile phone with you and ensure someone knows where you are heading. But my advice is to wait till the weather clears up. You'll enjoy the walk more then as well.

Although the walks follow existing rights of way, the choice of routes is entirely my own. Therefore, you will need to follow my directions carefully, to ensure that you don't go off course, and more importantly that you do not trespass on to private land. For additional reassurance, you may wish to keep a map with you. For the city/town walks a street plan will suffice but when venturing into the country, the best maps are the Ordnance Survey Explorer maps which are designed very much for the needs of walkers and cyclists. You may also wish to supplement my (necessarily) potted notes about features of particular interest with further books and guides. My suggestions for further reading are:

David Bathurst – *Walking The Coastline Of Sussex*, SB Publications 2002
Joanna Billing (ed.) – *The Hidden Places Of Sussex*, Travel Publishing Ltd 2000
Arthur Cooke – *Off The Beaten Track In Sussex*, Herbert Jenkins (nd)
Patrick Coulcher – *Unto The Hills*, Book Guild 2001
Iain Finlayson – *Writers In Romney Marsh*, Severn House 1986
Ken Green – *Chichester – An Illustrated History*, Breedon Books 2002
Simon Jenkins – *England's Thousand Best Churches*, Allen Lane 1999
Esther Meynell – *Sussex*, Robert Hale 1947
Paul Millmore – *The South Downs Way*, Aurum Press 1996

INTRODUCTION

Ian Nairn and Nikolaus Pevsner – *Sussex (Buildings of England Series)*, Penguin 1965
John Rackham – *Brighton Ghosts, Hove Hauntings*, Latimer 2001
Keith Spence – *The Companion Guide To Kent And Sussex*, Companion Guides 1999
Jeff Vinter – *Railway Walks – GWR & SR*, Alan Sutton 1990

It just remains for me to wish you very happy walking and, if you think there are better contenders in any of the categories, or can think of other categories round which a good Sussex walk can be based, don't hesitate to let us know!

David Bathurst
Christmas 2002

Chapter One

Best Railway Walk

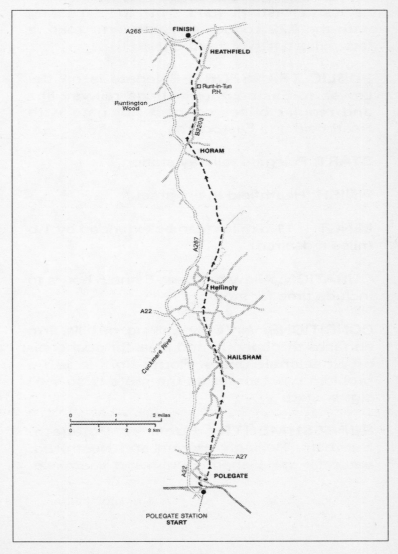

ACCESS BY CAR: Polegate is just off the A27 Lewes to Hastings road, close to its meeting with the A22 London to Eastbourne road, a few miles north of Eastbourne.

PUBLIC TRANSPORT: Polegate is on the Lewes to Eastbourne/Hastings railway line and regular buses connect Polegate with Heathfield and Eastbourne.

START: Polegate railway station.

FINISH: Heathfield main street.

LENGTH: 11.5 miles (can be extended by 1.5 miles if desired)

DURATION: Allow between 5 and 6 hours to include time for stops.

CONDITIONS: Very easy walking, no hills, firm surfaces throughout, and ideal for pushchair or wheelchair users. Route-finding is no problem whatsoever as the route is so well signposted.

REFRESHMENTS: Pubs at Polegate, Hailsham, Hellingly, Horam and Heathfield, and cafés at Hailsham, Horam and Heathfield.

One of the most encouraging environmental trends of recent years has been the conversion of disused railway lines into footpaths and cycleways, providing not only excellent recreational opportunities but an opportunity to revisit our industrial past and take us back to the time when the country railway did indeed provide the principal means of communication between smaller towns and villages. A number of stretches of disused railway are open to the public in Sussex, but the Polegate to Heathfield line, known affectionately as the Cuckoo Line, is in my view the most satisfying and interesting as well as being quite superbly maintained. It passes through a wide variety of landscapes, many of its original features have been restored and/or preserved, and it is extremely easy to follow.

The original line between Polegate and Hailsham opened in May 1849, with the extension from Hailsham to Heathfield opening in April 1880. A further extension, on to Eridge near Tunbridge Wells, was opened in September 1880. The line was cheaply constructed and had a number of steep gradients and sharp curves. It was certainly busy: in 1961/62, just a few years before closure, there were 24 northbound and 25 southbound trains every day. Sadly, the line fell victim to the Beeching axe, with passenger services north of Hailsham ending on 14 June 1965, freight services to Heathfield ending in April 1968 and the death knell sounding for the Polegate-Hailsham line on 9 September 1968. While virtually all of the section north of Heathfield has remained in private hands ever since, and out of bounds to walkers, the section south of Heathfield has developed into an excellent path, aided by substantial cash injections from the local council. The improvements have been comparatively recent: as short a time ago as 1990 Jeff Vinter, chairman of the Railway Ramblers, was writing of the 'muddy morass' north of Polegate and the fact that 'wellington boots will remain essential until the ... work programme is complete.' Those whose wellingtons have still not recovered from their punishment can only seethe when they see modern walkers ambling along the new concrete paths in trainers, flip-flops and stilettos.

Beginning at Polegate station, turn right out of the station approach road and go up the main street. The village is modern and nondescript, its only feature of note being the windmill and museum some distance away. Proceed up the street to its end, turning right at the T-junction onto Station Road then shortly left into School Lane. As the lane bends to approach the school buildings, you continue on in a straight line to join the so-called Cuckoo Trail which will follow the course of the old Cuckoo Line all the way to Heathfield, signposted here as 11 miles away. Almost immediately you begin to reap the benefit of the council's investment in this leisure facility: modern, colourful signposting, firm concrete surfacing, and lineside benches with woodcarvings that are always artistic and sometimes almost surreal. It is almost impossible to put a foot wrong.

Proceed confidently northwards, emerging from the outskirts of Polegate into open country, but almost at once having to cross the brand new A27 Polegate bypass. The traffic noise from this stays with you for some time. However, the surroundings do become more rural for a while; tall vegetation borders each side of the path, and a signboard tells you of some of the bird life and wildlife to look out for including, naturally, the cuckoo in the spring.

An early chance of refreshment comes with a tearoom within a mill complex that also contains a craft centre just to the right of the path. You rise to cross Summerhill Lane – note that road junctions and bridges are all signed, using an appealing green motif that is reminiscent of old station signboards in times past – and then at the next road junction a pedestrian crossing is provided. Note the crossing-keeper's cottage to your left, just over the road.

The going beyond the crossing is initially straightforward, but just as you are getting into your stride, you find the path widening into Freshfield Close, and you are directed right into Lindfield Drive and left again into Station Road, with a pleasant lake to your right. Continue on up Station Road, now approaching the centre of Hailsham. Pass the Railway Tavern then, just before reaching the top end of Station Road, turn left as signposted, off the road and down to an underpass just to the right of the skateboard park. If you wish to visit Hailsham, simply carry on to the end of Station Road and cross over into North Street, which in turn leads to the High Street. Although it is quite a sprawling town, Hailsham maintains a sturdy rural character and a certain gentility and charm: it boasts a thriving cattle market, its High Street contains some good Georgian buildings, there is a fifteenth-century church with a tower built in chequers of flint and squared stone, and there are plenty of good shops, pubs and cafés. It was once a thriving centre of the rope industry, and allegedly supplied cords used in prisons for executions.

Now back on the course of the old line, you go through the underpass and all is straightforward for a while. You go under the impressive Teinicks Bridge, a fine piece of brickwork, and then the less pleasing Eastwell Place Bridge, and the functional and wholly unappealing London Road Bridge. You are now moving away from the centre of Hailsham, but still have to negotiate a large modern housing estate. Initially you skirt the right-hand edge of it, but are then forced through the middle of it, though in fairness a path is provided for walkers. You have to cross one of the residential roads, shortly afterwards leaving the estate, then pass under the Hawks Road Bridge which feels more like a small tunnel than a bridge. There is a definite suburban feel as you continue to the very busy Upper Horsebridge Road, where again a pedestrian crossing, controlled by lights, is provided for you. Once over this road, you at last leave Hailsham behind, and now embark on six miles of really magical walking – old railway walking at its best.

You now head for Hellingly, and, as you approach the village, look out for a most extraordinary wooden sculpture consisting of naked bodies. Delights of a more traditional kind are soon at hand, though, with the magnificently preserved old Hellingly Station building, complete with canopy, and just under the next road bridge, you will find signs to the Golden Martlet pub as well as easy access to the village. It is a pretty place with a twelfth-century church that boasts a fine gilded organ and Early English north transept and chancel. Hellingly Station really came into its own in 1899 when work started on constructing the huge East Sussex Asylum, later to become known as Hellingly Mental Hospital, which was completed in 1903. To facilitate the conveyance of passengers to the hospital from the main line, a branch line was constructed, running from Hellingly Station to the hospital. The line, which was electrified, ceased to carry passengers in 1931, but freight traffic continued until March 1959, the freight consisting of coal which was used for the hospital's boilers and generators which in turn provided power for the electric locomotive.

Beyond Hellingly you drop down to cross Mill Lane, and shortly go over a modest-looking river. This is in fact the Cuckmere, the estuary of which is one of the most picturesque and impressively unspoilt features on the Sussex coast. You continue through quite glorious countryside, with fields and woodland on both sides, and a real sense of tranquillity. There is a really nice feel to this part of the walk – the knowledge of being on a clear, well-marked path with no route-finding problems, enjoying lovely unspoilt scenery which will not have changed since passengers viewed it from their train windows a century or more ago. There are even one or two numbered posts that are clearly relics of the old line.

You pass under Shawpits Bridge and the impressive triple-arched Woodhams Bridge, and over the delightfully-named Cattle Creep Bridge, the path now in the shade of woodland that is splendidly refreshing and cooling on a hot day. The woodland surrounding the path seems to thicken as you approach Horam. Sadly, as at Hailsham, the path temporarily peters out into a modern housing estate. Unlike at Hailsham, however, you need only proceed a short distance before seeing the Cuckoo Trail signposted and in no time you are on your way up the old line again. A signpost indicates you have left Polegate 9 miles behind – somehow it seems less. A signpost also points the way up to Horam's main street, effectively a right fork off the course of the Cuckoo Trail but proceeding virtually parallel with the trail itself. Turn left at the T-junction at the end to continue your detour into Horam.

The village is pleasant – there is a good shop and a transport café which should satisfy your appetite and your thirst – but unremarkable save for the large cider press by the main road which belongs to the makers of Merrydown cider. Unlike at Hellingly, there is no trace of the station which at various times has been known as Horeham Road for Waldron (Waldron being a hamlet a few miles away), Horeham Road and Waldron, and Waldron and Horeham Road. Try remembering and reciting that after a visit to the Merrydown cider press …

Just two miles remain before Heathfield is reached. There is a contrasting scene to the left and right: to the left, delightful rolling fields and woods, and to the right, the busy B2203 road, the noise of which undoubtedly mars the peace and timelessness of your journey. You drop to Tubwell Lane, then continue over Maynards Green Bridge and the less than elegantly named Runts Farm Bridge (note that nearby there is marked on the map a Runtington Wood and a pub called the Runt-in-Tun); the path gets a little further away from the B2203, and the rural feel temporarily returns. Some steps have been created in the small cutting to your left, giving access to a picnic area, a most delightful spot with beautiful views. Beyond the picnic area there is a bench with the word IDEA carved into the woodwork. It is all most mysterious. Are they the initials of the carver? Or did he just think it was a good idea?

Moving swiftly on, you arrive at New Ghyll Road. You cross over, and proceed to plain Ghyll Road, having to descend to cross it. You are now in the sprawling outer reaches of Heathfield, among trim but uninteresting modern housing, virtually all of which appears to post-date the demise of the old railway. Your path proceeds in determined fashion through the seemingly endless modern development, but then appears to give up the struggle, the path broadening out into a car park. Keep following the Cuckoo Trail signposts for Heathfield centre, crossing over one road then reaching a T-junction with another. Turn right onto the road, but very shortly turn left onto a path that leads through a children's play area (the site of the old, long since demolished, station buildings and platforms) to the undoubted climax of your journey, Heathfield Tunnel. This is now open to the public and is well illuminated throughout, although your walk through the tunnel still feels like a bit of an adventure –

especially if water is dripping from the roof down to the ground, as it was on my visit. Pass through the tunnel, entering what is known as Millennium Green, a small country park with a variety of recreational paths in and around the surrounding woodland. This is the end of your railway walk.

By forking right onto a path very soon after exiting from the tunnel, and climbing, you soon gain access to Heathfield's main street via the Co-op car park. Heathfield is an uninteresting place, but its main street offers all the amenities a tired and thirsty walker might hope for, including a good bus service back to Polegate. If, however, you feel this is an anticlimactical end to your journey, you could follow the main street eastwards for roughly half a mile then turn left and follow a minor road to Mayfield.

Once served by the old railway, Mayfield is a beautiful village with some fine timbered buildings, and the remains of a palace which was one of the great residences of the medieval Archbishops of Canterbury. Polegate-bound buses stop in Mayfield as well. You may even seek out a bus from Heathfield to the nearby village of Burwash, another picturesque place whose main attraction is the magnificent Batemans, the sometime home of Rudyard Kipling. Your other option, on reaching Millennium Green, is to follow the path onwards rather than forking right as directed above; you are of course still on the old railway and can continue on it for well over half a mile, passing through beautiful woodland. It is ironic that just as you are getting into your stride again after picking your way through Heathfield that you reach a forbidding high fence that precludes further progress, with no obvious means of continuing. Perhaps one day it will be possible. But for now all you can do is turn back and go back the way you came – unless you, like me in the days before disused railways became more walker-friendly, have cultivated above-average vaulting skills and are prepared for your clothes to invite the attentions of the native brambles and your legs the voracious appetites of the indigenous canines.

Chapter Two

Best Town Walk

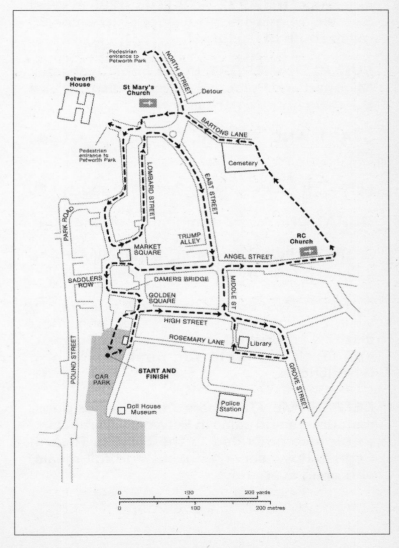

ACCESS BY CAR: Petworth stands at the junction of the A272, A283 and A285 in West Sussex, 14 miles north-east of Chichester, 20 miles south of Guildford.

PUBLIC TRANSPORT: Buses from Chichester, Midhurst and Pulborough. Very limited service Sundays and Bank Holidays.

START AND FINISH: The main car park, Petworth.

LENGTH: Approximately 2 miles in aggregate.

DURATION: Allow a minimum of one hour, but, depending on the number of stops, it could be five times that, especially if you include a tour of Petworth House.

CONDITIONS: Extremely easy. A good family walk or evening stroll. Save for one short stretch, metalled surfaces throughout, eminently suitable for pushchairs and wheelchairs.

REFRESHMENTS: There are numerous pubs, restaurants and cafés in Petworth. Particularly to be recommended is the Sadlers Rest in Sadlers Row, serving snacks and full meals, and open every day.

What is the most attractive town in Sussex? There are many contenders: Lewes, Arundel, Rye, Midhurst and Steyning could all lay claim to the title. But in terms of richness and variety of architecture within a very confined area and easy accessibility to the walker, combined with excellent shops and refreshment opportunities, I would suggest that Petworth outranks them all.

Referred to as 'Peteorde' in the Domesday Book, it has changed very little over several centuries. In her book, *Sussex*, Esther Meynell writes: 'Stone walls and stone paving still give to Petworth its comfortable air of solidarity, and though the general aspect is that of a little eighteenth-century town in the seemly proportions of numbers of the house fronts, yet many of the irregular roof lines and jutting angles, combined with the narrowness of some of the streets [...] suggest a much older Tudor Petworth.' It still has a number of elements of an ancient feudal settlement with its old centre and great house separated by a wall.

Petworth was once an important market town with a long history: the market square is believed to originate in the thirteenth century, and its street fair began as long ago as 1189. Between the fourteenth and sixteenth centuries the town was noted for its cloth weaving, and many of the fine houses that remain today once belonged to merchants. Although inevitably many of the old family businesses have gone, there are still plenty of traditional small shops and there is a reassuringly timeless feel about it, with an atmosphere that is more suggestive of a bygone age than the twenty-first century.

Inexorably linked with the Percy, Egremont and Leconfield families (Lord Egremont occupies Petworth House, the central building in the market square is called the Leconfield Hall and many of the houses have been part of the Leconfield estate) it was once an important town with Quarter Sessions and a prison, and boasted its own railway station. A magistrates' court sat here until as recently as 1994. It is now more renowned as an antique centre, but visitors also come from long distances to see its undoubted jewel, Petworth House, standing in magnificent parkland. Some also travel here to enjoy the big arts festival which takes place here every July and which has attracted many big names.

Petworth's real problem is its very limited accessibility by public transport: five minutes too long spent admiring one of the masterpieces in Petworth Park may mean the difference between proffering a return ticket for the homeward bus journey, and digging deep into one's pocket for an unforeseen and unwelcome taxi fare.

Your walk begins in the town's central car park. Make for the public toilets at the top end of the car park and follow an alleyway past the right-hand wall of the toilet block, heading for the town centre. Immediately you notice Lancaster House to the right, a fine building of red brick and mellow stone, with a lovely secluded garden. The garden is said to be the hiding place of church silver in Cromwell's day, while the house was the home of a Lord of a local manor. Part of the house is now a florist's shop. Just past Lancaster House you reach Golden Square and turn right into the High Street. Immediately on your right as you proceed up the High Street is Charles Hennings, a vintners' shop with huge champagne bottles adorning the windows.

You pass the red brick Kitchen Court, and a row of attractive mellow stone cottages on your right, while the half-timbered Riverbank is opposite on the left. Just beyond Pannell's Cottage on the right, turn off to the right to visit The Cottage; note the shed painted with flowers and a tiny enclosed cottage garden. When I visited in May, this contained a riot of forget-me-nots. Beyond, look straight ahead to a wall and weathervane, behind which is the cream-walled Rosemary Cottage, while to the right and below is Holly Cottage guarded by plentiful greenery. Back on the High Street, you pass a fine array of white houses including Westbury, Bradleys and the half-timbered Corral; opposite is Tiffins tearoom with its red-painted interior walls and low beams. It is perhaps a little too early in the walk to be thinking of refreshment, but if you do feel you have deserved it, you will not be disappointed. On my first visit to the tearoom I spotted a very tempting array of cakes on display and was on the point of making my selection only to be told in no uncertain terms that they were not for consumption as they were too old. Refreshing honesty to go with my refreshing brew.

Next door to Tiffins is the blue-painted Annette Puttnam building; look out for the reassuringly old-fashioned Hovis sign. Continue past the magnificent cream-walled Fairfield House and the delectable sixteenth-century half-timbered Fairfield Cottage. Pass the Middle Street turning, noting the Old Forge to the left, while opposite is the fine tile-hung Windmill House. The name is a reminder that hereabouts was a large area containing storehouses and cottages associated with a working windmill. Then on the left you reach the Petworth Cottage Museum. This is a reconstruction of a Leconfield Estate cottage as it was in 1910, although the cottage itself dates back to the seventeenth century. In 1910 it was occupied by a seamstress at Petworth House named Maria Cummings, a widow with four grown-up children. The museum provides a fascinating insight into cottage life as it was in the early years of the twentieth century, from mundane matters such as cooking and washing to moments of relaxation with the newspaper. It is open every Wednesday to Sunday afternoon plus Bank Holidays from April to

October and is well worth a visit. Immediately adjoining it is the wisteria-clad Ricketts Cottage, then Cobblestones and Quoinstones – can you spot the oriental character in the garden?

Continue uphill, noting two long rows of cottages to the left with their massive chimney stacks. They date from the mid-Victorian age and provided homes for the large numbers of employees of the Leconfield Estate. On the right are two impressive houses, Stone Croft and Stone House with very imposing steps and doorway: for many years Stone House was lived in by ministers of the Congregational Church. Take the next right into Rosemary Lane, but before you do, look down to Grove House ahead of you with its timbers adorning the side wall. The principal buildings of Rosemary Lane are the Royal British Legion house to the right, and to the left two formidable edifices which remind us that this has been a busy workaday town – the severe redbrick magistrates' court, and, further down, the police station which dates back to 1835. You are now at the top of the town and there is a nice view to the rooftops and vegetation of the lower parts of the town and, on a clear day, to the attractive rolling countryside beyond including the South Downs.

The magistrates' court, which continued until the mid-1990s, was right up to its closure a busy court dealing with a good deal of serious crime, but its facilities were a little on the primitive side. On many occasions the first application made to the magistrates was for advocates to be allowed to keep their coats on in court, and whenever there was a heavy rainstorm the patience of all those in court would be tried by the banging of the raindrops or hailstones on the roof above.

Turn right off Rosemary Lane at the library, passing to the left of the library and descending past the fine Fairview

House. This is a lovely part of Petworth where time does seem to have stood still. The alleyway takes you back to the High Street. Turn left and almost immediately right into Middle Street. Much of Middle Street has hardly changed in four hundred years, and the street has many splendid buildings: to the left, as you walk along it (note the Oxo sign too), is the brick and timber house occupied by Rod Wilson Antiques, and to the right are further pretty buildings including the attractive Keytes, Kitts Willow and Alfreston House. Colours of the walls include yellow, pink and blue.

At the end of Middle Street, turn right into the narrow Angel Street – do take care as you walk, as there is no pavement and traffic does move quite fast along it. There are some austere red brick houses to the right to begin with, but to the left, a little further down, is the early eighteenth-century Angel Hotel and the green-painted Angel House with the date 1626 inscribed on it. Just beyond that is the tile-hung Old Walls Cottage – note the slightly protruding lower storey! Further down to the left is the 1896 Roman Catholic Church. Don't continue along the main road, but bear left by the church, following the track bearing the 'No Through Road' sign, and descend to a gorgeous viewpoint overlooking acres of unspoilt countryside, a lovely surprise so close to the bustling town centre, and another indication of the town's remarkable compactness.

Turn left through a wooden 'turnstile'; though primarily designed to deter cyclists, it is not particularly pushchair or wheelchair friendly either, and if you find it impossible to negotiate your pushchair or wheelchair through it, it is necessary to backtrack along Angel Street, turning right into East Street and arriving at the church where you may pick up the route again. Assuming you do get through, follow a concrete path, keeping the sensational views to the right, but noting also some commemorative trees by the path which were planted for the Queen's Silver Jubilee in 1977.

Soon you reach a gate, where you swing left and go uphill past another turnstile to enter Bartons Lane. Pass a small cemetery, where generations of the Egremont family are buried, and Glebe Cottage to the left – you have to envy the occupiers the view they get from their window! – while to the right are walls bedecked with a tremendous display of wallflowers. At the end of Bartons Lane, on the corner at the junction with the main road, is the Coach House with a notice on the wall proclaiming that a reward of five shillings will be paid to anyone who gives information leading to the conviction of those who throw stones. One wonders who the last person was to be rewarded in this way ...

If you wish to visit Petworth Park, turn right out of Bartons Lane along North Street, the main A272 highway. This is extremely busy, and again care is needed especially when crossing the road. Admire the fabulous timbers above Pandora's Box, the fine late-eighteenth-century redbrick North House and the impressive doorway to Preyste House. Beyond these stand Somerset Hospital, an early seventeenth-century brick house that was converted to almshouses in 1746. Over the road is the Cowyard, giving pedestrian access to the 700-acre Petworth Park.

If you want to miss the Park, cross the road at the end of Bartons Lane and head into the churchyard opposite, proceeding to the main entrance of St Mary's Church with its lofty and curiously un-English red-brick tower which was topped as comparatively recently as 1953. The church boasts a thirteenth-century chancel and a fourteenth-century north arcade, and several monuments of which arguably the most eye-catching is the life-size figure of George, Third Earl of

Egremont, dating from the nineteenth century. It was sculpted by Edward Hodges Baily, who also sculpted the statue on top of Nelson's Column. In the baptistry below the chapel there is a communal monument to the Percy family, founders of the Northumberland dynasty. Eleven Earls of Northumberland lived in the 'old' Petworth House between the fourteenth and the seventeenth century. The ninth Earl, Henry Percy, was nicknamed the Wizard Earl for his interest in science and alchemy, and was suspected of having a part in the Gunpowder Plot. He was imprisoned in the Tower of London and was only released on payment of the sum of £11,000, which even today is a great deal of money.

Emerge from the church by the main entrance/exit, looking right for a fine view of Petworth House, and go straight down the church path to the road, not back to Bartons Lane. On reaching the road, turn right to follow it. Just before the road swings left, you will arrive at the entrance to Petworth House. Though the house dates back more than six centuries, little of the original work remains apart from the chapel. Wholesale rebuilding took place between 1688 and 1696 by Charles Seymour, 6th Duke of Somerset, with an exterior that has been likened to that of a French chateau. The Duke's descendant, the 2nd Earl of Egremont, completed the construction of the house. Today it contains a magnificent collection of paintings, with works by Turner, Rembrandt, Gainsborough, Van Dyck and Holbein. Of particular interest is the Grinling Gibbons Room, with many superb examples of Gibbons' unbelievably intricate carvings. Other highlights are the Marble Hall, Grand Staircase, Turner Room, the Sculpture Gallery where many fine paintings and excellent sculpture work can be admired, and the chapel with its remarkable woodwork.

The grounds, including the deer park, were landscaped in the mid-eighteenth century by Capability Brown. Although

Petworth House is very close to the centre of the town, and might be said to glower down at it – Daniel Defoe wrote that it 'stands as it were with its elbows to the town' – to enter it is to enter what seems like another world. Esther Meynell observes: 'The great towering walls and spiked gateways that guard Petworth House from any contact with the common people have an air, in these days, not only arrogant but absurd – the helmeted stone coat-of-arms, ludicrously pompous, on the gate-posts speak of eighteenth-century intolerance, and recall monumental effigies of the same period where bewigged landed proprietors are received in Heaven by effusive and servile angels.'

Return to the road and follow it; as stated above it swings sharp left just beyond the entrance to Petworth House. Again there is no pavement here, so take care. As you go, note the austere 1887 Ebenezer Chapel, which still advertises services at 11 a.m. and 2.30 p.m. Immediately beyond the chapel, and with some relief, you take the very next left, noting the pretty Ormonde Cottage on the corner, and the not so pretty Market Square garage on the other side! Follow this road, passing a very good Tourist Information Office, to Market Square, Petworth's focal point. It is the site of one of the last remaining street fairs in southern England. To your left is the magnificent Natwest Bank building.

You may wish to linger in Market Square but the walk continues by your turning left up Lombard Street. As you turn left, look straight ahead at the wisteria-clad building which now houses a firm of well-established solicitors; there are good examples here of windows that were 'stopped' to evade the notorious Window Tax of the mid-eighteenth century. Lombard Street, which was once one of the busiest shopping streets in the town and boasting a variety of trades including haberdashery, grocer, butcher and baker, is one of

Petworth's finest. Pevsner describes Lombard Street as 'one of the best picturesque streets in a county that is full of them.' Look out on the left-hand side for the Lombard Street Gallery and Lombard House, while to the right is the impressive redbrick Lombards Café Bar, and Pettifers which dates from 1573 and is almost Cotswold in character, boasting superb mullioned windows. One lovely touch can be seen above Bacchus Gallery with its sign, appropriately enough, depicting figures carrying bunches of grapes.

At the end of Lombard Street, turn right into Church Street (the church is straight ahead of you) and then immediately right again into East Street. Pause to look at the obelisk built at the junction of Church Street and East Street; it was designed by Sir Charles Barry as a token of thanks to Lord Leconfield for giving gas lighting to the town. As you begin your walk down East Street, note on the left-hand side the splendid Georgian redbrick George House, dating back to 1805, and further along the street are some excellent half-timbered buildings, one housing a gunsmith's and one containing the Tudor Rose Antiques Centre. Denman's is described by Pevsner as probably the best half-timbered house in Petworth.

You pass a cobbled courtyard leading to Jevington Court, and soon reach three more gems: The Leads, a mid-eighteenth-century brick building, Stringers Hall with its bay windows and dating back to the middle of the seventeenth century, and Daintrey House, a huge Georgian mansion, albeit containing some Elizabethan features, and boasting magnificent gardens. Pevsner describes it as 'the most ambitious house in Petworth'.

Turn right at the end of East Street into New Street, now heading downhill; note the row of houses to the left with a different coloured door on each one. Look out for the splendidly old-fashioned menswear shop a little further down. Soon you find yourself back in Market Square. In the centre of the square is Leconfield Hall, built in 1794 and formerly a court house. Pass to the left of the Hall, continuing on in a straight line from New Street, turning left at the end. Your route is first left at the end into Damers Bridge, but you may wish to detour first right into Saddlers Row. This street contains the 1899 Swan Hotel although this has now been converted into shops and flats. You may however, wish to make a beeline for my favourite eating place in Petworth, the convenient and very pleasant Sadlers Rest restaurant/café/tearoom. Its building dates back to 1481 and has served as a saddler, barber, wigmaker, stationer, sweetshop and greengrocer. One of its specialities, which I suspect may not have survived the recent change of ownership, used to be a delightful confection known as 'No Cook Chocolate Cake'!

Follow Damers Bridge, passing the United Reformed Church which is on the left, and soon you find yourself back at Golden Square. Note Avenings opposite the United Reformed Church on Golden Square, which dates back to 1770. Turn right, passing a traditional butchers' shop which offers such delights as haggis, Scottish black pudding and mealy white pudding, and then bear right into a courtyard with a modern shopping complex which includes a lovely delicatessen on the left-hand side. You emerge into the car park to conclude your walk. It is then that the compactness of Petworth becomes a distinct advantage; it will take you just a few minutes, if that, to stroll back to the Tourist Information Office to find out how many hours – or days – you will have to wait for the bus home.

Chapter Three

Best Village Walk

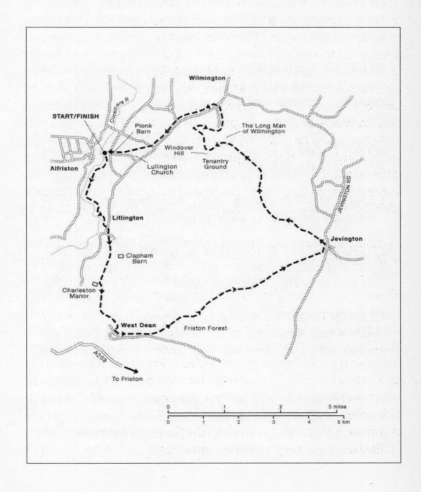

ACCESS BY CAR: Alfriston is on a minor road between the A27 Lewes-Eastbourne road near Berwick and the A259 at Seaford. There are car parks in the village.

PUBLIC TRANSPORT: Limited bus service from Lewes and Eastbourne. Berwick, the nearest railway station, is over 2 miles from Alfriston.

START AND FINISH: The green in front of Alfriston Parish Church.

LENGTH: 9.5 miles (can be shortened to 8 miles by omitting Wilmington).

DURATION: Allowing a good 3-4 hours' walking and ample time for village exploration, set aside a day for this walk.

CONDITIONS: Superb downland walking with a fair amount of up-and-down work, but some easy riverside and forest walking as well.

REFRESHMENTS: Numerous pubs and tearooms in Alfriston; pubs at Litlington, Jevington and Wilmington; tearooms at Jevington and Wilmington.

Sussex has so many pretty villages. Bosham, Findon, Lindfield, Burwash, Brightling, Ditchling, Rottingdean, Mayfield and Alfriston immediately spring to mind as examples of delightful village communities with a rich variety of architecture. I have chosen the last of these, Alfriston, as the start and finish point for a tour of five wonderfully unspoilt villages. Each has a magnificent downland setting; each is rich in history; each is predominantly built of flint, that most traditional of Sussex building materials; and each contains at least one significant attraction for the visitor, with three of them meriting considerable exploration.

The journey itself, linking the five villages, is quite outstandingly attractive, providing a huge variety of walking. You will walk beside a river, along the edge of rolling fields, through large areas of woodland, and along open downland tracks offering magnificent views to the surrounding countryside and the sea. And you will meet a Hungry Monk and a Long Man.

You begin at Alfriston, in front of the parish church on a spacious and lush green, with the delights of Alfriston village centre just a couple of minutes away. Alfriston, standing beside the picturesque Cuckmere River, has been described as the capital of the Cuckmere Valley; it was founded in Saxon times and was once an important port and market town. In its centre is a market square (it is actually more of a triangle) surrounded by shops and houses with fine brickwork, timber frames, tile-hanging and weatherboarding. The market cross in the square is one of only two left in the county, the other being at Chichester. Of particular interest in the village centre is the early-fifteenth-century Star Inn, the timbers of which are ornamented with carvings of beasts, and one carving is believed to depict St Michael and the dragon. At one corner of the inn stands perhaps the village's most memorable feature: a large red lion which was once the figurehead of a seventeenth-century Dutch ship. The Star was built early in the fifteenth century, probably as a rest house for pilgrims on their way to Chichester Cathedral to see the shrine of St Richard.

In the square is another old inn, the Market Cross Inn, also known as The Smugglers. At one time it was the home of Stanton Collins, leader of the successful Alfriston Gang who used Cuckmere Haven to land their booty. The inn had as many as six staircases. Nowadays the gangs that roam Alfriston are likely to be tourists; the lovely old buildings on the main street make it a popular place for visitors, who are well catered for by the profusion of eateries and tearooms. One of the tearooms, looking out on to the square, is also a music shop, selling not only musical gifts but a massive range of 'nostalgia' CDs and tapes, and so scones, jam and cream can be consumed to the accompaniment of marvellously catchy melodies that remain in the mind long after tea is over.

The two real historical gems of Alfriston are away from the village centre: the church of St Andrew, and the Clergy House that stands beside it. The Clergy House is a thatched and timbered building that has the distinction of being the first property to be acquired by the National Trust, for the princely sum of £10. Built around 1350, and lived in by vicars in medieval times, it is a superb example of a fourteenth-century Wealden hall house, and has been sensitively and skilfully renovated. Around the house is a fine traditional cottage garden containing many unusual flowers. The floor of the house has recently been relaid in the traditional Sussex method, with chunks of chalk rammed down and sealed with sour milk.

The fourteenth century church, with its magnificent

riverside setting, has become known as the Cathedral of the South Downs. Its stonework of small, square knapped flints is a rarity for a church in Sussex, and its cruciform design is attributed, according to tradition, to the sight of four oxen lying down in the shape of a cross when it was being built. Up until the 1930s, shepherds would be laid to rest here with a scrap of raw wool in their hand, to inform St Peter that their poor church attendance was as a result of caring for their flocks!

You may be quite reluctant to drag yourself from Alfriston to start walking, but reassure yourself that you will return to it later in the day. To begin your walk, bear left from the front of the church as you look at it, and follow the green to the banks of the Cuckmere, turning left and almost immediately arriving at the footbridge. Cross the bridge and then turn right onto a footpath, running alongside the river on a modest embankment. You are now following the course of the South Downs Way. This path can be muddy in winter, but the surroundings are delightful, with the waters of the Cuckmere to the right and peaceful meadows to the left. Dragonflies, damselflies and swans can all be seen here.

In less than a mile, the buildings of our next village, Litlington, come into view. Your path seems to be making a beeline for them, but then swings right, through a gate, and shortly swings left on what is now a metalled surface. Very soon you arrive at the road and the centre of Litlington. Litlington, like Alfriston, has Saxon origins, and although it lacks the charisma of Alfriston it is still a charming unspoilt place with a character of its own, and a magical setting with the Cuckmere meadows on one side and the steep-sided Downs on the other. It possesses a number of very attractive flint, stone and brick houses and gardens; one particularly prominent building, from which an excellent view is available from the waterside walk from Alfriston, has a plain stone top half and a flint bottom half. One of the larger properties, Clapham House, is the house where Maria Fitzherbert is supposed to have lived before she secretly married the Prince Regent, the future George IV, in 1785.

Litlington's focal point is the church, dating back to 1150, with its spire and white weatherboarded bell turret; both the nave and chancel are Norman, and until its restoration in 1863 it hardly changed at all. Despite being so small, the village is blessed with two excellent refreshment opportunities, the pretty Plough and Harrow pub, and the Tea House which first opened over 100 years ago. The atmosphere here is absolutely timeless and you can still enjoy tea served in most traditional fashion. On one visit ten years ago, I was fortunate to eat my tea with a puppet show going on in the garden.

From the metalled path, turn right onto the road, pass the Plough and Harrow, then as the road bends sharply right, take the track leading off to the left. Very soon you arrive at a South Downs Way signpost pointing at a path leading off to the right, and you join this path. You climb quite steeply through a field, and at the top you will enjoy a fine view to the right, with the buildings of Clapham Barn to the left. Continue along the South Downs Way, swinging slightly west of south, following the left-hand side of a hedgerow on what is quite a rough grassy path. Ahead of you are the trees of Friston Forest.

Now you begin to descend, dropping quite steeply to a T-junction of paths, meeting a wider track at the foot of the hill, with steep wooded hills rising up in front of you. Turn left onto the wider track. To your right here is Charleston Manor, which has its origins in Norman times – it is believed to have been built for the cupbearer of William the Conqueror

– and retains some Norman features although it has been added to over the years. It has a particularly fine garden with parterres and terraces divided by yew hedges.

Following the track away from the manor, you remain in the valley only briefly, before bearing right – still on the South Downs Way – and climbing a stepped path, now in the forest. On reaching the top you simply keep to the path, observing South Downs Way signposts, ignoring tracks leading off to the right and left, and in due course the houses of Westdean become apparent to your right. You reach a T-junction of paths and turn right to descend to the village, then turn left onto the main village street which contains the church.

Westdean is one of the most unspoilt villages in Sussex, its flint cottages, high flint walls and large barns sheltered by the beeches of Friston Forest. The flint-built rectory dates from the thirteenth century, and retains the interior shutters which were in use before glass was fitted in its windows. Close by is All Saints Church, which dates back to Norman times; inside is a bronze memorial to Lord Waverley who as Sir John Anderson introduced the air-raid shelter which bore his name. King Alfred is thought to have had a palace here, probably on the site in the village centre where the ruins of a medieval manor house and nearby dovecote are preserved as ancient monuments. South Downs Way walkers starting their pilgrimage from Eastbourne and passing through Westdean may be encouraged by the thought that their next encounter with Alfred will be his statue at Winchester – 92 miles distant. Perhaps 'encouraged' is the wrong word?

Continue on past the church and Manor Cottage, then turn left to follow the Forestry Commission road, heading resolutely now into Friston Forest. The going is fairly bland to begin with, but improves in just under half a mile, when the track forks, and you follow the left fork, with a signpost marked Jevington. Signposting in the forest is excellent, and simply by following signs to Jevington you will not go wrong. The path is initially delightfully grassy underfoot, but very shortly you reach a T-junction of paths (no signpost) and turn left onto a wider stony track. This becomes grassier and rises to reach a gate. Pass through the gate and go straight ahead, temporarily emerging from the woods to enjoy superb views across open countryside to the left. Soon you reach another gate, and pass through this gate to re-enter the forest.

Soon you reach another T-junction of paths; turn left and simply proceed along this path. The woodland is quite delightful and not the least claustrophobic, and you should watch out for a very attractive patch of coniferous woodland to your left as you make progress. At length, the path emerges from the wood for the last time, and you are treated to fantastic views to the downland around Jevington, your next objective. Progress is fast and easy as you plunge downhill, arriving at a road when you reach the bottom. Turn left to reach the centre of Jevington. There is food aplenty available here with a pub, tea garden and restaurant which claims to be the place where banoffi pie was born!

Jevington is a small village but could be described as a typical South Downs community with its lichen-covered flint cottages and farm buildings clustering along a leafy chestnut lane against a backcloth of steep hillsides. Its most historic building is the flint-built church, which boasts a Saxon west tower and also some Norman and Early English work, although it suffered terribly from insensitive restoration in the nineteenth century. There is an unusual Saxon sculpture on the north wall of the nave, depicting the Resurrection. The celebrated physician Dr Russell, whose treatise on 'The Uses of Seawater, Both External and Internal' was indirectly responsible for transforming Brighton into a holiday resort, is buried in the churchyard. Monastery Field, opposite the church, is the site of a fourteenth-century monastic settlement devoted to the Saxon martyr St Lewinna.

Other buildings of interest in the village include Jevington Place, the Eight Bells Inn, and the Hungry Monk restaurant, which not only boasts itself to be the birthplace of banoffi pie, but was the home of Jevington's most infamous resident, James Pettit, known as Jevington Jig. As well as being the village innkeeper he was a smuggler, working in collusion with the then church rector and other characters including Rook the Highwayman and the splendidly named Cream Pot Tom – although everyone in the village participated. The rectory cellar was a favoured place to store illegally imported goods, and many other houses in the village contained hideaways for contraband. Pettit frequently found himself in trouble with the law, receiving some harsh sentences including 7 years' transportation for stealing 2 hams of bacon in 1793. Somewhat surprisingly he was charged with stealing in this country in 1796 – had he escaped or successfully appealed? – and the jury took so long to reach their verdict that the judge shut them up without heat or light until they did so.

You now leave Jevington following the South Downs Way again, but this time you are on the bridleway alternative linking Eastbourne and Alfriston. Just after passing the Hungry Monk, turn left off the village street along the road leading to the church. Immediately before the church, turn left to follow the path, rising steadily under the shade of horse-chestnut, elm and ash. In just over a quarter of a mile from Jevington the path levels out at a junction of bridleways; go straight over the first crossroads and then bear left at the ensuing T-junction, noting one of the old-fashioned South

Downs Way plinths at this point. You follow a broad track, still in the trees and rising steadily, then emerge from the trees and immediately you will see a path leading off to the right. When I walked this section in summer 2002, there was no signpost here but the route of the South Downs Way, and our Best Village walk, does indeed turn right here, heading north-westwards towards Windover Hill. You continue to climb on a clear path, and can now enjoy tremendous views to the sea, both to your left and the right; the houses you can see beside the sea to your right are at the eastern end of Eastbourne. As you continue, however, the best views to the sea are to your left, with glorious downland scenery in between.

You continue to follow the South Downs Way, swinging from north-west to north, then more resolutely north-west again. The actual path is very narrow, but the way is obvious, and you will undoubtedly prefer to remain on the springy turf. Almost without warning the ground falls away dramatically to your left and you find yourself describing a rude semicircle round the top rim of a very steep grassy hillside with a dry valley beneath known as Tenantry Ground, swinging south-westwards. You are now on Windover Hill and as high as you are going to get, although the path curves round to the left of the summit plateau with its long barrow. By now the path has widened considerably and is a broad stony track.

You swing sharply northwards and begin to descend, keeping the summit plateau to your right, and reach a T-junction of paths. Turn left, then almost immediately fork right onto another path, leaving the South Downs Way. [NOTE: You could shorten the walk by a mile and a half and miss out Wilmington, simply following the South Downs Way to the road crossing marked * below.] You continue to descend but very shortly reach a gate to your right, through which you pass to follow a path which proceeds below Wilmington Hill. Soon you will see the giant hill figure known as the Long Man Of Wilmington to your right, and as you get up level with it you arrive at a gate through which a path goes off to the left. Go through the gate and follow this path downhill to the road. Just before the road, turn right to follow a footpath that goes parallel with the road to reach the village of Wilmington.

Wilmington's two most impressive features are the ruins of a Benedictine priory, and the Long Man, which looks rather better from a distance. The surviving buildings of the priory, founded soon after the Norman Conquest, include a thirteenth-century hall, gatehouse and enclosed courtyard. The Long Man is almost 250 feet high, and the largest such representation of a man in Europe; he holds what appears to be a staff in each hand. During the Second World War it was covered up, as it was felt that the white chalk might be a navigation aid to German bombers. The origin of the Long Man is a mystery, with evidence to suggest it could back to Saxon, Roman or even Bronze Age times, but it has been conceded that it might just be the work of an artistic monk from the priory!

The village also boasts a part Norman and part Gothic church which was connected by a cloister to the priory; in the churchyard is an enormous yew tree which may well be as old as the church itself. Its trunk is 23 feet in girth and poles are used to support its boughs. The church itself contains a pretty weatherboarded and shingled bell turret, a Norman chancel and a splendid Jacobean pulpit complete with sounding board. The village street contains a happy mixture of flint, brick, thatch and medieval timber; some timbered cottages date back to the fifteenth century while Chantry House, of flint, brick and thatch, boasts a grotesque face with bulging eyes on its exterior wall. It is a pity that the Wishing Well Tearooms, housed in a building that dates back 250 years, are right at the other end of the village, but you will at least know you have earned your cuppa, especially after all that banoffi pie in Jevington.

To return to Alfriston, you must retrace your steps. Follow the road back to the path leading down from the Long Man, but now continue along the road, heading south-westwards, for just over a mile. The road is reasonably quiet, and there are good views to the Long Man to your left and the escarpment of the Downs below Firle Beacon to your right, so this is not an unpleasant walk. In about a mile from Wilmington the road rises to meet the South Downs Way which crosses the road here [*If you have decided to cut out Wilmington you will be reunited with the main route at this point]. Turn right onto the South Downs Way but almost immediately bear left through a gate onto a path which heads downhill through an open field. To your left, across the field, is Lullington Church, one of the smallest in the country with room for about 20 people – it is actually the chancel of a much larger building, and contains some fourteenth-century work. It is worth detouring to it from our route.

Our route continues downhill to reach a T-junction with a wider track; a left turn leads to Lullington Church, but our way is right, very soon arriving at a road, passing the splendidly named Plonk Barn. Turn right onto the road then immediately left onto a path that very shortly arrives at the footbridge where you began. Cross the bridge and turn left onto the riverbank, then right to find yourself back on the church green at Alfriston. The combination of hard walking and good eating will certainly earn you a good night's slumber, enlivened no doubt by visions of the Hungry Monk doing a Jevington Jig on the Long Man ... or is it the Hungry Man doing a Charleston on the Long Monk ... who said Sussex villages are sleepy?

Chapter Four

Best Woodland Walk

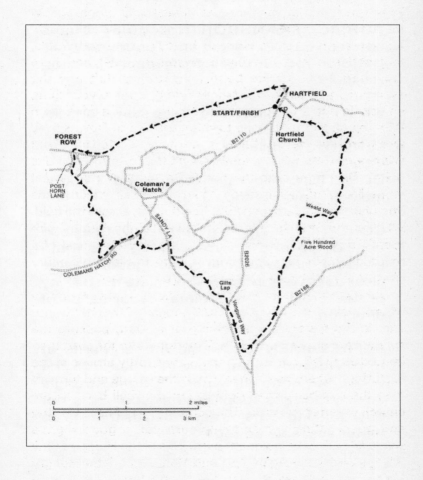

ACCESS BY CAR: Hartfield is on the B2110 Forest Row – Tunbridge Wells road.

PUBLIC TRANSPORT: Regular buses between East Grinstead and Tunbridge Wells (regular rail services from each) serving Hartfield.

START AND FINISH: The village store, Hartfield.

LENGTH: 15 miles.

DURATION: Allow between 6 and 7 hours, including picnic stop.

CONDITIONS: This is a long trek, with a good deal of up and down walking; the main problem, however, will be navigation. A fine clear day is essential to appreciate the beauty of the forest and to maintain your sense of direction.

REFRESHMENTS: Ample refreshments at Hartfield and Forest Row (4 miles into the walk), but none elsewhere. You are strongly advised to take supplies with you. On a hot day, drinking water is essential, as there is no water available en route.

BEST WOODLAND WALK

Sussex is richly blessed with woodland but, in my view, Ashdown Forest offers the most rewarding such walking in the county for its variety, its fantastic views and its literary and historical associations. For lovers of children's literature, the forest will be forever associated with A. A. Milne's world of Winnie-the-Pooh, for it was Ashdown Forest that inspired the adventures of everybody's favourite bear. The forest also has a long, although not always happy, history. This 14,000-acre tract of woodland and heathland, once part of the massive forest Anderida that covered south-east England, lies on the high ridges of the Weald, equidistant from the North and South Downs, and comprises the lowest strata lying beneath the huge chalk dome that once covered Kent and Sussex. It is triangular in shape, with Forest Row, Crowborough and Maresfield making up its corners. It was once a royal hunting ground, favoured by sportsmen for its large deer population, although long before the hunters arrived prehistoric man had created trackways over it, the Romans had built a road across it and commoners living on its edges had rights to enter the forest to gather wood for fuel. A famous sporting owner was John of Gaunt, who was Duke of Lancaster, and the forest thus became known as Lancaster Great Park. There were frequent conflicts between commoners endeavouring to assert their rights, and both hunters and landowners wishing to improve their parcels of land within the forest. However, the demand for fuel for the area's iron industry caused many of the trees to be cut down (not for nothing has it been nicknamed Bashdown Forest!), and by the middle of the seventeenth century the deer had gone completely.

The area subsequently underwent something of a renaissance, with clumps of Scots pine trees being planted in the nineteenth century, the deer returned, and a Board of

Conservators was established in 1885 to properly administer the forest and resolve competing claims. By the late twentieth century it had become a major tourist attraction, with walkers and drivers coming to admire its largely unspoilt beauty, although it suffered extremely badly during the Great Storm of 1987. Ashdown Forest today offers a huge variety of landscapes, with some thickly forested areas and some tracts of bare heathland, combining to provide a paradise for the walker and nature lover – and, of course, Winnie-the-Pooh worshippers.

Much of the wooded area of the forest is silver birch, but there are many other trees to be found: not only the Scots pine, as previously mentioned, but also beech, mature sweet chestnut, alder, hazel and oak. Beeches were particularly badly affected by the 1987 storm, but a large number of old pollarded trees survive. Bracken grows in the forest in profusion, as does gorse, which can be seen in flower almost all the year round. Heather is abundant, particularly ling, and so is purple moor-grass; one unusual plant to proliferate in the forest is the red fly agaric toadstool, while the moister parts of the forest may yield bog asphodel and marsh gentian. There are many different animals, birds and insects to be seen in the forest: foxes, fallow deer, roe deer, badgers, wood warblers, woodpeckers, stonechats, woodmice, pipistrelle bats, sparrowhawks, Dartford warblers, tree pipits, kestrels, blue butterflies, emperor moths, dragonflies and common lizards. Adders may also be found in the forest; they are of course poisonous, but very nervous of man – if that is any comfort!

There are precious few amenities within the forest area, and I therefore choose to start this 'best forest walk' in Hartfield, a most attractive village just outside the forest boundaries, but which, in contrast to the stark remoteness of parts of the forest offers all the creature comforts one could ask for. The village does have two obvious links with the forest, being an old hunting settlement and boasting a shop called Pooh Corner offering every conceivable type of Winnie-the-Pooh memorabilia. A. A. Milne lived in Cotchford Farm, just outside the village, and wrote the Pooh stories to entertain his son Christopher Robin. The Pooh Corner shop is in fact 300 years old and was a sweet shop to which young Christopher was taken by his nanny. Incidentally, the original Poohsticks Bridge lies just a few miles from the village but is not on our route. It is identified on many OS maps and is easily accessible.

The village itself contains many delightful buildings, many of traditional weatherboarding, and fronted by magnificently kept gardens. The church, with a spire that is an impressive landmark for miles around, has late-thirteenth-century features, while the upper floor of the early-sixteenth-century timber-framed cottage called The Lychgate in fact extends above the church lychgate. Among the best houses in the main street, besides Pooh Corner, are the sixteenth-century Hay Wagon Inn, where we begin, and the seventeenth-century Stairs Farmhouse that was owned by Adam Faith in the 1970s.

Proceed northwards from the village store, following the main street. Having left the shops and pubs behind, the main road bends right but your way is straight on along the road signposted Edenbridge. The road goes downhill, and then rises to cross a bridge. Having descended with the road you do not ascend with it, but fork right onto a paved path that goes down to the Forest Way, the course of an old railway. Turn left and go under the old railway bridge to begin an easy 4-mile walk along the old railway track. This was formerly the East Grinstead – Tunbridge Wells railway, formed by the East Grinstead, Groombridge and Tunbridge Wells Railway Company and operated by the London, Brighton and South Coast Railway. Failure to comply with official requirements meant that although work began on the line in July 1863, opening was delayed four times and when it was finally opened on 1 October 1866 the local press was so tired of waiting that they did not report it.

The line as far as Groombridge became a casualty of Dr Beeching and closed on 1 January 1967, almost exactly a century after opening. Bradshaw's timetable of 1890 shows six trains plying the route between Hartfield and Forest Row each day, the first leaving Hartfield at 7.43 a.m. and the last at 6.30 p.m. Passengers travelling the other way and just missing the 9.43 a.m. from Forest Row would have to wait until 1.35 p.m. for the next one! Forest Row was the busiest intermediate station between Tunbridge Wells and East Grinstead and in the final years of the line a number of London commuters were using the station.

One bizarre incident in the line's history was in June 1868 when a driver hauling a cattle train near Hartfield was warned of a bull on the line. As luck would have it, the axle of one of the trucks broke, causing a derailment. The bull heard the sound of the female cows in distress, and raced towards them with such speed that the driver, hurrying for the refuge of his footplate, broke his collar bone!

The walk along the track is lovely, and is very suitable for pushchairs and wheelchairs. Although you are not yet officially in Ashdown Forest, there are many patches of woodland in view amongst the rolling pastures and meadows, and the line itself is frequently in the shade of trees, providing welcome shade on a hot day. The views from the embankment are delightful and constantly changing, and it is no surprise that the track is a very popular leisure facility, so watch out for dogs, cyclists and pushchairs.

At length, you become aware of traffic noise to your left, following the main Hartfield – Forest Row road. You then pass under two very imposing overbridges in fairly quick succession, and notice houses lining the route to the left, with some paths actually running from the line up into the gardens! Just before a row of distinctive modern red houses, built at right-angles to the track on the left, there is an obvious exit path, the first since the build-up of houses began. Leave the track at this point and take this path to reach the main road.

By turning right you will reach the main centre of Forest Row, where buses can take you back to Hartfield if you wish to break at this point. Forest Row is a sprawling place but it has an attractive centre with many old buildings and a stone wall commemorating a visit made here by President John F. Kennedy. More pertinently, perhaps, Forest Row offers the very last opportunity for a drink or to restock your rucksack – so don't say you weren't warned …

The walking thus far has been very easy but it now becomes extremely fiddly for a while as you enter Ashdown Forest. Follow the instructions carefully. On reaching the main road, go straight over into the residential Post Horn Lane and follow it to its end where it meets Primrose Lane on a sharp right-hand bend. At this point, go straight on along a metalled drive heading straight for the golf course.

Royal Ashdown Forest is one of the most prestigious and also scenic golf courses in southern England. Access across the course is not prohibited for walkers but it should go without saying that you should not encroach onto the tees or greens, and you should try to stick to paths beside the fairways wherever possible. The golf course obtained its royal title after the Duke of Cambridge, who had commanded the troops at a review on the Forest by Queen Victoria, had been prevailed upon to drive a ball wearing his full dress.

A short way up the drive you will see a sign stating 'Ashdown Forest – Speed Limit 10 mph'. Fork left here onto a path that initially runs roughly parallel with the drive through the trees. The metalled drive then veers away to the right but you continue uphill in the same direction, keeping carefully to the path and ignoring turnings off. You emerge from the trees and pass just to the right of a tiny pond, reaching a T-junction with a sandy track. Turn right onto this track then almost immediately left onto a grey stony track. Follow this past the fifteenth tee of the golf course, then continue to follow it over a fairway – the track is barely recognisable across the fairway itself – and on, still along the track, to reach another metalled driveway at its end. Turn right onto the driveway and follow it until you reach a driveway going off to the left. You take this left turn and shortly reach the fairway of the thirteenth hole. Cross it, then turn left to follow beside it, going downhill then up to the thirteenth tee by means of a path.

This is the start of a most pleasant walk right beside the golf course; as stated previously, there is no difficulty of access and in fact this is a most agreeable part of the walk, with the lush green fairways beautifully complementing the heathland and patches of woodland. Turn right at the thirteenth tee, and proceed beside the twelfth hole, keeping the fairway to your left and crossing the area of heather between tee and fairway. Turn left to pass round the back of the eleventh green then bear right to follow along the right-hand side of the tenth fairway up to the green. Bear right here to follow the track heading for the eleventh tee. Just before you reach it, turn left up a narrow but well-defined path that climbs steeply away from the golf course. As you leave the course, you may wonder why you haven't seen a single bunker. That's easy – there aren't any on the course at all. One for the dreaded Christmas trivia quiz, perhaps …

Proceed up the narrow path and arrive at a crossroads of paths at the top. You turn left to continue, but there is a seat at the path junction, and you may well feel you've earned a rest here. Sit awhile and enjoy a fantastic view across the northern part of the forest, and the Wealden countryside beyond; suddenly that old railway line, though barely two and a half miles distant, seems an awfully long way away! As stated, proceed away from the path junction, heading north-eastwards along a path that passes through the woods parallel with Colemans Hatch Road; you can hear the traffic noise on this busy road as you go.

You go over a number of crossing paths and tracks, but in due course – roughly half a mile from the viewpoint seat – you reach a crossroads of paths where ahead to the right is a break in the woodland in the form of a field. Turn right at this crossroads and proceed to the road. Cross more or less straight over onto Sandy Lane, a no-through road with signs to various properties. [If you wish to break the walk in two, and/or have had enough, don't go across into Sandy Lane but turn left onto the road, and follow it, soon forking left to the hamlet of Coleman's Hatch which is on the bus route between Forest Row and Hartfield. Do check bus times in advance!]

Proceed along Sandy Lane for a few hundred yards, passing the cricket pitch which is on your left, and ignore also a right fork, then immediately beyond the pitch turn left along a well-defined woodland track. Proceed along the track, now enjoying fine views to the southern part of the forest. Ignore paths leading off to the left just beyond the cricket pitch, and a right fork as the path descends; continue roughly eastwards, going over a crossroads of paths, and arrive at a T-junction with a wider track. Turn left onto this track and follow it down to a road. You have all this time, from Sandy Lane onwards, been following the Vanguard Way, a long-distance footpath, but you would never guess it, for throughout my walk along this section I saw not a single signpost for it. Had the Vanguard Vandals been at work?

Turn right onto the road and proceed for another few hundred yards, looking out for a ford on your left. Cross the bridge beside the ford (you can paddle through if you insist!) and continue briefly up the road beyond, but almost immediately turn right onto a track heading uphill. You are now into the second half of the walk, and approaching the best section of all. Your track climbs steadily, and in just under half a mile bends quite markedly to the left. Soon after this left bend you reach a crossroads of paths, with a clear track going off to the right. Take this right-hand turn and follow the track, still rising and ignoring paths leading off to the right and left. It is wonderful walking, not too strenuous, with superb unspoilt countryside all around you. Though you are surrounded by ample woodland, with some particularly fine conifers close to the track, there are also numerous breaks and open spaces which prevent the closed-in sensation that some forest walking can give.

At length you reach the top of the hill, the ground levels out and you arrive at a T-junction of paths. A seat is provided here; it is a perfect place for you to stop, enjoy the refreshing drink you thoughtfully purchased before the start, and gaze out across miles of breathtaking countryside. Your way is right, southwards, but not far north of here is Gills Lap, the inspiration for Galleon's Leap, one of the places mentioned in A. A. Milne's work. To attempt, however, to seek out Owl's

House, Eeyore's Gloomy Place, the Bee Tree, and the Pooh Trap for Heffalumps would take up more time than is realistically available on this visit. And you'll certainly be wasting your time trying to ascertain Where The Woozle Wasn't …

At the 'seat' junction you turn right, and head towards a car park partially screened by a very large clump of trees. Your track aims for the left of the clump then bends sharp left to skirt the north edge of the car park and reach the B2026 road just north-east of its junction with the minor road with which you have been going very roughly parallel during your recent climb. Cross straight over the B2026 to join a track which, happily for navigational purposes, runs virtually parallel with this road, heading south-eastwards. You are on some of the highest ground of Ashdown Forest, on a breezy open landscape with sweeping views over miles of countryside, partially wooded but also with many wide open spaces. It is tremendous walking, providing the weather is good, but in wet weather, especially walking into a southerly wind, this could be a real slog.

Ignore two or three tracks branching off left, but in a little under a mile from the car park, you will reach a track going off left with a post inscribed WW. This indicates the Wealdway, another long-distance path which is mercifully much better signposted than the Vanguard Way is (things may have improved by the time you read this book!). Turn left at the WW post to follow the Wealdway, which will be your companion for all but the final mile and a half of the journey. From this reassuringly wide track there are now tremendous views away to your left. You are now in what is known as Five Hundred Acre Wood, the 100 Aker (sic) Wood from the Winnie-the-Pooh books. This was originally planted with beech and oak in the eighteenth century in an enclosure created in a decree made in 1693 and owned by Earl de la Warr. It was particularly badly affected in the Great Storm in 1987.

After about half a mile, watch for a wide track coming in from the right; ignore the next left turn after this, but you do take the following left turn, marked by a Wealdway signpost. Tremendous walking now follows on a good clear path, descending slightly, with magnificent views to your left. A signpost marks a left fork you should take, and shortly thereafter you turn left at a T-junction of paths, following the path and ignoring a left fork you soon reach. The way ahead is obvious; don't let the lack of Wealdway signposts alarm you. You are now descending rather more purposefully and the woodland around you is perceptibly thicker, but this is still tremendous walking. You should in due course reach a T-junction of paths at the north end of the wood, with open fields stretching ahead of you. If you don't, panic, and reach for the compass. If you haven't got a compass, draw in your breath slowly, count to ten … then panic.

Assuming all is well, turn right onto a track which leads downhill. At the bottom of the hill, look out for a sweet little pond to the left. Here, bear right onto a metalled drive. There follows an ascent that seems somewhat inhuman after the long descent you have just done, and it is quite a relief to swing left at the top of the hill and descend. You pass some buildings which lie to the left of the drive, and soon approach another driveway with which your drive forms a T-junction. Shortly before it, though, there is a slipway giving more immediate access to it. Follow it down to meet it, only to be confronted with a severe 'Private Drive' sign immediately ahead of you. Watch for a footpath going off to the right of the private driveway; follow this initially along the flat then uphill, and you are soon reunited with the driveway but on the north side of a private property. At last you have left the forest.

Now it is plain sailing for a while as you follow the driveway for the best part of a mile. This is all a bit anticlimactical, and you are probably longing for a refreshing pint in Hartfield; the good news is that if you look to the left you should be able to see the church spire poking out of the trees. Watch carefully for a sign pointing left to Old Buckhurst. Shortly beyond that is a stile with a High Weald Landscape Trail waymark on it; go over the stile and follow the clear path through the field. At the end of the field, go over another stile into a wood, then at the ensuing T-junction of paths turn left and almost immediately right, over a footbridge. Once over the bridge, fork right immediately, and proceed along a clear track, noting the showjumping field to your right.

A pleasant walk follows, the track rising slowly but surely, passing through rolling pastures but with patches of woodland close by, albeit very tame compared with what has gone before. Soon you get a super view of Hartfield Church to your right. Watch carefully for a stile also on your right – this again just under a mile from the showjumping field – bearing the High Weald Landscape Trail waymark. Go over the stile and proceed, very shortly turning right at a further stile to emerge by the church. Turn left onto the road here and you will shortly be back on Hartfield village street. Here you can blow all the money saved by the absence of refreshments en route with a meal in one of the eateries along the village street, still have change for a jar of Winnie-the-Pooh honey, and then head home on the bus wearily trying to remember the second line of Cottleston Pie.

Chapter Five

Best Heritage Walk

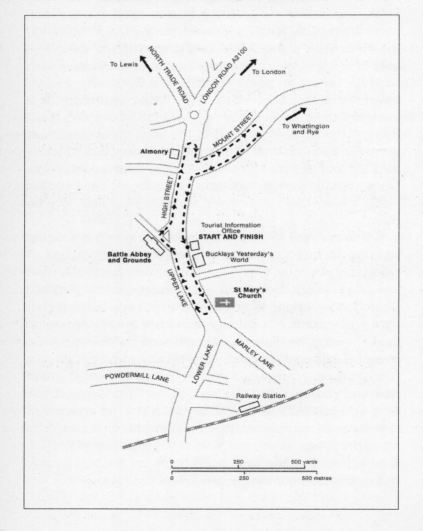

ACCESS BY CAR: Battle is reachable from the A22 at Hailsham via the A271 or from the A21 main London road just south of Robertsbridge via the A2100.

PUBLIC TRANSPORT: Excellent rail services on the London–Tunbridge Wells–Hastings line.

START AND FINISH: Tourist Information Office, High Street, Battle.

LENGTH: Minimum 1 mile; could be longer depending on the amount walked within the grounds of Battle Abbey.

DURATION: Allow a full day to enjoy the many exciting things on offer.

CONDITIONS: Very easy – street walking throughout.

REFRESHMENTS: There are numerous pubs and cafés in Battle.

If there is one place in Sussex that encapsulates England and the English over the past millennium, Battle is that place. This is the shortest walk in the book, yet on your brief perambulation you will discover England in a nutshell: you will learn of the last invaders of England and the impact of the invasion on English culture, you will see many different types of English architecture, both sacred and secular, you will enjoy many typically English institutions from cosy bookshops and ancient inns to old-fashioned tearooms, and you will see an exhibition that celebrates everyday English life throughout the last century and a half. You may even get some typically English weather – so take your umbrella just in case!

Battle was, of course, the site of the historic conflict in 1066 between Harold, the Saxon King of England, and William, Duke of Normandy. The invading Normans were victorious and brought sweeping social and cultural changes to England, the legacy of which is still evident today nearly one thousand years later. It is fitting that your walk should start at the Tourist Information Office just over the road from Battle Abbey, built by William the Conqueror on the very spot where Harold fell. You will come to this in due course, but for now, turn left out of the Tourist Information Office and proceed along the continuation of the High Street known as Upper Lake.

Almost immediately you pass Yesterday's World, which you will return to at the end of the walk. Go on along this road until you reach the Norman church of St Mary The Virgin, a beautiful historic church that is typical of so many in Sussex and indeed England. It was founded by Abbot Ralph in the early twelfth century and was enlarged towards the end of that century, with the west doorway following a little after that, and a west tower that was built in the fifteenth century. There are some impressive memorials in the church, including the brasses to Sir John Lowe and William Arnold dating back to the early fifteenth century and the recumbent effigies of Sir Anthony Browne and his wife who died in 1548.

Having left the church, cross the road and head back towards the town centre. If you have come here by train, you could just pick up the walk from St Mary's Church having accessed it via Station Road and Lower Lake, perhaps after sampling another aspect of English life in the form of curling British Rail sandwiches on your outward journey.

As you make your way back towards the town centre, you arrive very shortly at the entrance to the Battle of Hastings Battlefield and Battle Abbey, owned by English Heritage. By paying the admission fee, not only will you get to see the battlefield and abbey ruins, but you will be able to take an interactive audio tour of the battlefield with contributions from Aelfric, a Saxon soldier, Henri, a Norman knight, and Edith, King Harold's mistress, describing from their eyes the story of what really happened on that red-letter day, 14 October 1066. There is also a video introduction, the Prelude to Battle exhibition, and a museum on abbey life.

As stated above, the abbey was built by William, in atonement for the blood he shed on the battlefield, and the accommodation provided for those who built the abbey constituted the beginning of the town of Battle. The gatehouse itself, where you pay to enter the complex, was built in 1338, although there is earlier work in the western wing and in the various arches you can see examples of Norman, Gothic and early Renaissance architecture.

Continue round Abbey Green, passing the magnificent Pilgrims Rest, a half-timbered building that dates from the fifteenth century; with its leaded lights in the windows, it can be said to be a classic Medieval construction. Very nearby, moving on round the Green, is the tile-hung seventeenth-century house, a tearoom called A Taste Of Battle, serving delicious afternoon teas, while just a few houses further along is Nick Whistler Art & Books. This is a lovely old-fashioned bookshop, with a wonderfully eclectic array of stock crammed into a very small space – the sort of bookshop from which it is a pleasure to buy a book, even if you do see the same volume sitting in the city discount bookstore two days later for a fiver less.

Having left Abbey Green, continue now up the High Street, passing the splendid Natwest Bank and Italian restaurant next door in a building which dates back to 1700, and proceed to the Sue Ryder shop. This fine tile-hung building is thought to be the oldest ironmonger's in the country, starting up here in 1680. Continue on to the Bull Hotel, an inn that dates from the seventeenth century and is built of ashlar masonry salvaged from the Abbey kitchen, and this is closely followed by Friar House. The house, with its timber framing and its steeply sloping roof, dates back to 1642, the year of the outbreak of the English Civil War. Not only is there a working pottery, but upstairs you can also see some of the weaponry of the Civil War era.

Another excellent timber-framed house a little further on is the Almonry. This was originally a five-bay hall house built in the fifteenth century, but it has been partially rebuilt since, with chimneys being among those features added in the sixteenth and seventeenth century. It is likely to have got its name because it was constructed on ground set aside for the use of the Almoner of the Abbey. Afternoon tea in the Almonry is a most pleasant experience, with generous slices of coffee gateau and Victoria sponge served with pots of tea inside the old building and in the courtyard.

Emerging from the Almonry, cross the road and begin

walking back down the High Street on the other side of the road, but turn left into Mount Street. As you proceed up the left-hand side, look out for the building with three distinctive arches and a curious tower set upon the roof. This was once an industrial building and was used by a blacksmith. Today the premises are occupied by Friday Ad!

There is a wonderful mix of architectural styles to be enjoyed as you proceed up Mount Street. It includes the weatherboarded Battle Wool Shop; the dental surgery still boasting the fire insurance plaque on its front; the robust red-brick Roman Catholic church of late-nineteenth-century origin, a real piece of Victoriana; and the early-nineteenth-century Zion Chapel, now the home of Battle Baptist Church. Cross the road and turn right, passing the splendid houses Slatters and Peppers, the latter bearing a plaque dated 1480, and the superb Kings Head, a masterpiece of tile-hanging, and the perfect place to sit and relax with a pint of traditional English beer or cider. It is also worth taking a brief detour to the car park off Mount Street on this side of the road to enjoy the beautiful views across the unspoilt Wealden countryside.

Return to the High Street, turning left and proceeding past another typically Victorian chapel, dating back to the early 1880s and boasting a particularly intricate doorway. It is now a grocery, which is not quite what the original architects had in mind. You pass an alleyway leading to Abbey Court – look up at the sign Newbery Preserves which reminds us that the Newbery Jam Factory started here in the latter part of the nineteenth century – and having passed the splendidly old-fashioned butcher's shop just beyond the alleyway, go forward to Langton House. This is the massive building which now accommodates both Battle Memorial Hall and the HSBC Bank. It began in the sixteenth century as a two-storeyed half-timbered building, another storey being built around

1700, a new front being added in the eighteenth century, and shop-fronts appearing in the twentieth century. There is a double doorway with its use of the Ionic Order, a fine example of classical architecture in the town.

Very soon you find yourself back at the Tourist Information Office, but hopefully you will still have ample time to enjoy Yesterday's World. Winner of the England For Excellence 2002 Visitor Attraction Of The Year, this is a wonderful place for discovering all the colours and flavours of yesteryear, with over 30 authentic room and shop settings housed in a medieval hall house, all designed to help find out what life was really like for our nineteenth- and early-twentieth-century ancestors. In the museum, you may navigate your way through Victorian Britain and the Edwardian era, going on into the twentieth century and culminating in the Swinging Sixties. Collections include Queen Victoria's personal effects and nightdress, and correspondence by Queen Elizabeth II. Attractions include the 1930s country railway station, a 1950s/60s TV shop, a 1950s cycle shop, a country garage, a 1930s hairdresser, a Victorian fudge marquee, and, if you're desperate, a Victorian water closet!

Emerging from Yesterday's World, you may wish to call into the adjoining nostalgic and contemporary gift shop which is attached to the museum but which costs nothing to enter. Though admission may be free, you could easily be tempted to snap up some of the many books, CDs, videos and cards that recall a bygone and, dare one say, less hectic and rather gentler age. Having emerged, laden with goodies, from the gift shop, you might wish to round off your walk in Battle with a visit to the Pilgrims Rest, which, you will recall, is the fine timbered building on Abbey Green and which offers delicious typically English afternoon teas. Savouries include quiches, jacket potatoes, roast meals, Welsh rarebits, ploughmans, and scones of many varieties including fruit, cheese, herb and celery, while for afters there is a sumptuous selection of cakes and a tremendous variety of leaf teas. Then, having feasted on the best of British for the day – our Norman ancestry, our Royal traditions, our architecture, industry, food, drink, countryside, trades, fads and personalities, all encapsulated into one very short walk – you can return to the station for the train home. Assuming, in the time-honoured spirit of stiff upper-lipped British optimism, you think it will turn up.

Chapter Six

Best Literary Walk

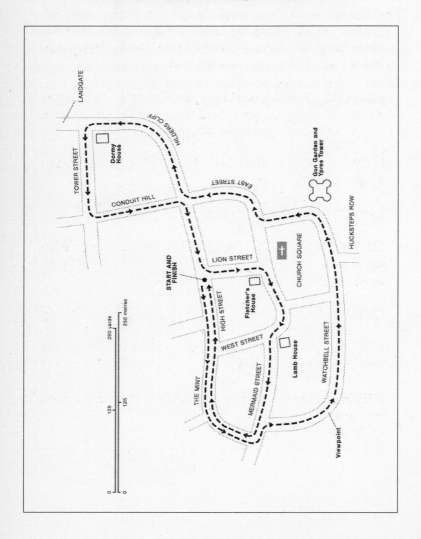

ACCESS BY CAR: Rye is on the A259 Hastings–Folkestone road, and the A268 from Hawkhurst; join the A268 from A28 (Ashford–Hastings road) at Sandhurst.

PUBLIC TRANSPORT: Rye is on the Hastings–Ashford railway line, and there are regular bus links to Hastings and Brighton.

START AND FINISH: Martello Bookshop, High Street, Rye.

LENGTH: Approximately 1.5 miles.

DURATION: Allow a full day to do justice to all the town has to offer in terms of historic and, in particular, literary interest.

CONDITIONS: Very easy – street walking throughout – but you will struggle to manoeuvre pushchairs and wheelchairs along the cobbled streets.

REFRESHMENTS: Numerous pubs and cafés in Rye.

Although this is a very short walk, it is a paradise for the literary historian, not least because of the historic beauty of the town of Rye where the walk is set.

Looking at Rye now, it is difficult to imagine that during the Middle Ages this hilltop town, formerly a hill fort, was almost ringed by water, standing as it did on a promontory and being guarded by two estuaries close to their entry into the open sea. Formerly it was an important port, exporting iron and wool to the continent, and in the mid-fourteenth century it became one of the so-called Cinque Ports, providing ships for the English fleet. A target for French aggression during the Hundred Years War, its fate as a port was sealed by silting, which left the town two miles inland. There are, however, numerous reminders of its prosperity: the town's narrow streets are crammed with fine old houses, many weatherboarded, tilehung or timberframed.

Arguably the town's focal point is St Mary's Church, the most intriguing features of which are the gilded cherubs who strike the bells of the tower clock. Among the many secular buildings of particular interest are the Mermaid Inn in the beautiful, cobbled Mermaid Street, containing thirteenth-century features, and the seventeenth-century Old Grammar School with its distinctive Dutch gables.

Reminders of the town's strategic importance are to be found in the fourteenth-century Landgate, the last remaining of the town's original three fortified gates, and the thirteenth-century Ypres Tower, once a prison and now a museum.

The combination of the wealth of history, olde-worlde charm, magnificent setting and proximity of the sea have inspired a large number of writers, including novelists, dramatists, biographers, poets, and writers of sports literature and children's fiction, to either live or stay here for some if not all of their writing careers, many drawing upon their love of the town and its surroundings in the course of their writing. As a literary pilgrim you will doubtless be delighted not only to follow in the footsteps of so many authors, but to be able to pick up copies of their work and that of countless others in the plethora of bookshops along the town's old streets. It may be that, despite it being so short, you can and will make the walk last all day, but you can be comforted that if you are pushed for time you can, wherever you are on the walk, be back at the car park in minutes.

Your walk begins at the Martello Bookshop in the bustling High Street, with its extensive range of shops and restaurants. One of the most famous authors associated with Rye, E. F. Benson, based locations in his *Mapp & Lucia* books on houses in Rye (the town in which these locations were situated became known as Tilling), and many of these are to be found in the High Street. On the north side of the street, the Mariners was the inspiration for Diva, later Ye Olde Tea House; numbers 18 and 19 High Street were E. F. Benson's Post Office; and number 21 was Mr Rice, Poulterer. A little further down, Barclays Bank was a stationer's in Miss Mapp's world. On the opposite side of the street, The George became the fictional King's Arms, number 97 was Twistevant's the greengrocer, number 99 Twemlow's the grocer, and number 100 was Worthington's the butcher. You will see more of the world of Mapp and Lucia later on along the way.

The Martello Bookshop is a wholly appropriate place to start a literary walk; although it stocks chiefly new books it is a deliciously old-fashioned shop with an excellent range of books written by authors associated with Rye. When I visited it had a fine E. F. Benson display and a good many of the works of Malcolm Saville, the hugely popular children's writer who lived in nearby Winchelsea but who set many of his *Lone Pine* adventures in the Rye area, and who wrote a very readable history of the town of Rye. You may also see Clive King's *The Town That Went South*, which was set in and around Rye, as were Thackeray's unfinished work *Denis Duval* and Ford Madox Ford's *The Half Moon* and early chapters of *Some Do Not*. In short, the shop is a browser's paradise. You might just decide to stay here and not bother with the rest of the walk at all!

Assuming you do wish to continue, turn right out of the shop and walk down the High Street, which swings to the left and becomes The Mint. At the end of The Mint, turn hard left into Mermaid Street. You will return to this wonderful cobbled street later, but for the moment take the first right up Traders Passage, a very narrow half-cobbled street which was the home of the linguist and prolific travel writer Eric Whelpton. His two autobiographical works, *The Making of an Englishman* and *The Making of a European* were largely written in Rye. You emerge into a more open area, with the Hope Anchor to your left and excellent views to the surrounding countryside opening up to your right, and you continue along the picturesque Watchbell Street, where the illustrator Mabel Lucy Attwell once lived.

Watchbell Street was the inspiration for Curfew Street in the E. F. Benson books, with the Hope Anchor renamed the Trader's Arms and Watchbell Corner becoming Suntrap; the attractive viewpoint close to the Hope Anchor was the Viewpoint Terrace of the *Mapp & Lucia* books. You go straight on into Church Square, continuing effectively in a straight line. Having passed beyond the lychgate, look very carefully for an extremely narrow alley to the right. This doesn't appear on the street maps of Rye but is clearly signed as Hucksteps Row. This is a private alley with a dead-end. At the end of it is the Forecastle, the sometime home of one of Rye's most celebrated literary figures, Marguerite Radclyffe Hall.

Born in 1886, she had already published four novels before she came to Rye in 1928 with her lesbian lover, Una, Lady Troubridge, to visit an acquaintance, and was instantly attracted to the town. It was just before she came to Rye that her fifth book appeared. Entitled *The Well of Loneliness*, it aroused huge controversy because of its pro-lesbian stance, and as a result of court proceedings the book was banned both in Britain and the USA. She and Lady Troubridge moved into the Forecastle and used Rye as the setting for a subsequent book, *The Sixth Beatitude*, with Rye being renamed Rother. The couple left Rye in December 1928, but returned in October 1929 and bought The Black Boy in the High Street; whilst it was being restored they put up at the Mermaid Inn (see below) and 8 Watchbell Street. Noel Coward was among their guests at The Black Boy. In February 1934 the two women moved back to the Forecastle and stayed until 1940, subsequently moving to Devon.

The relationship between them was not always smooth during their latter years in Rye, and was further complicated by an affair that Radclyffe Hall had with a White Russian, Evguenia Souline, which outlasted her time in Rye. Radclyffe Hall died in 1943, leaving a very considerable estate, her popularity as a novelist undoubtedly assured by the blaze of publicity attending *The Well Of Loneliness*. One can think of few more obvious incentives to purchase a book that *The Express* described as 'a book that must be suppressed' and the courts condemned as 'disgusting [and] prejudicial to the morals of the community'!

Beyond Hucksteps Row, continue to the far corner of Church Square, where you arrive at a T-junction. Your way is left, past the east walls of the church, but by detouring right you will very soon reach Ypres Tower which now houses Rye Castle Museum. Just to the left of the museum as you look at it from the corner of Church Square is Gungarden Lodge, the home of John Ryan who created one of the best-loved characters in children's fiction, Captain Pugwash.

Son of Sir Andrew Ryan, KBE, CMG, John Ryan was born in March 1921, served in the Lincolnshire Regiment in India and Burma during the Second World War, and after the war established a career as a children's author, illustrator and cartoon film-maker. He published 35 books including 19 *Captain Pugwash* titles from 1955 onwards, and made not only the *Captain Pugwash* films but over 100 others between 1956 and 1980, including *Sir Prancelot* and *Mary, Mungo and Midge*. Since 1964 he has also been cartoonist for the *Catholic Herald*. However, it is his fictional nautical characters for which he is most famous. They first appeared in the *Eagle* magazine and then in book form from 1957, and were seen in a *Radio Times* comic strip in the 1960s. Pugwash, described as 'an entertaining if unsubtle descendant of Captain Hook', thinks himself 'the bravest, most handsome pirate in the Seven Seas' but in actual fact he is a total coward, and Tom, his cabin boy, is the only person with initiative and sense on his ship *The Black Pig*. The arch-enemy of Pugwash is Cut-Throat Jake, and it is Tom who saves his master time and again. The stories are given special appeal by Ryan's verbal wit and eye for comic incident as well as his beautifully detailed drawings. Though the books are written for children, adults also can appreciate much of the artwork and verbal humour: typical is the name of the head of the British Navy, Admiral Sir Splycemeigh Mainbrace!

John Ryan is not the only writer to have lived in this part of Rye: another scribe who established himself at this corner of Church Square, at number 38, was Patric Dickinson. Like Bernard Darwin, about whom more below, Dickinson, who was born in 1914, wrote a good deal about golf, and his book, *A Round Of Golf Courses*, is a well-respected and oft-quoted golfing guide. However, he is best known as a poet. After the Second World War, he joined the BBC as a trainee but became Features Producer and subsequently Drama Producer, and was in effect the Corporation's Poetry Editor, meeting or corresponding with every significant poet of that time. His own poetry included collections entitled *Theseus And The Minotaur*, *Stone In The Midst And Other Poems*, *The Sailing Race*, *The Scale Of Things*, *The World I See*, and *This Cold Universe*.

It was in the spring of 1947 that Patric Dickinson and his wife Sheila bought a property in Church Square for the palindromic figure of £2855.8s.2d. He left the BBC – the award to him of an Atlantic Award in Literature was under the condition that he gave up his job there – but continued to do freelance work for them, with his literary feature on the poet Ernest Dowson being broadcast at the very same time that his son David was born. He also continued to write poetry, and the Martello Bookshop published his collection entitled *Poems From Rye* with his acerbic comments about the constant stream of tourists in the town: 'Through our streets the morons shamble asking for Woolworths [...] / They pile our streets with litter and fag-ends, too-fat adults and kids / Slurping ice-cream as they lurch on the cobbles, gawping and peering ...'

Continue past the east walls of the church, soon reaching the north-east corner of Church Square. Turn right into East Street and follow this past the Flushing Inn down to the High Street. Turn right along the street, which between here and the Landgate (alluded to above) is known as Hilders Cliff, arriving shortly at a viewpoint with telescope. I say 'shortly' but between Church Square and this point you will almost certainly be tempted into the secondhand bookshops along the way.

Continue past the viewpoint to the Landgate, but just before the Landgate on the other side of the road is a house that is described on its nameplate as Old Dormy, otherwise known as The Dormy House. One of the most celebrated residents of The Dormy House was the golf writer Bernard Darwin, who was a regular contributor to *The Times* and whose book, *Golf Courses Of The British Isles*, is one of the best golfing guides ever written. His description of Deal golf course, on the coast of the adjoining county of Kent, is typical of his work: 'The larks seem to me to sing a little louder and more cheerfully there and the grass to have a more poignantly delicious taste of garlic.' He wrote many other books including *Green Memories, Golf Between Two Wars, Golf, War on the Line, The World That Fred Made, Out Of The Rough* and *Playing The Like*. He also found time to play a lot of golf and was for many years a member of Woking Golf Club in Surrey; it is said that on one occasion, after missing his fourth short putt on the fourth green he rolled in agony on the turf, biting it as he went, and cried, 'And now, God, perhaps you are satisfied!'

Go past the Landgate then shortly turn left into Tower Street and bear left again up Conduit Hill, arriving back at the junction of East Street and the High Street. Turn right to follow the High Street then turn left up Lion Street, heading straight for the church. Secondhand books and afternoon teas are in plentiful supply along this street. As you get near the church, you pass (or possibly enter) the Simon the Pieman tearoom, which has been in business since 1920 and is the oldest established tearoom in Rye.

Immediately beyond on the right you will arrive at the fifteenth-century timber-framed Fletcher's House, another tearoom and the birthplace of the dramatist John Fletcher in 1579. He is said by some to be the sole son of Rye to have achieved a lasting reputation, his work playing a significant part in the development of both the tragicomedy and the comedy of manners in the seventeenth century. It was probably as one of Ben Jonson's circle that he became introduced to Francis Beaumont in London, and collaborated with him in such plays as *The Philaster*, *The Maid's Tragedy* and *A King And No King*, which were extremely successful. Later he was to collaborate with Shakespeare in the writing of Henry VIII and *The Two Noble Kinsmen*, and he wrote many plays on his own, with such intriguing titles as *The Faithful Shepherdess*, *The Mad Lover*, *The Wild Goose Chase* and *A Wife For A Month.*

Continue up to the church. You turn right immediately in front of the church to continue your walk, but I strongly recommend that you break off your literary walk to see the inside for yourself, and climb up the tower to enjoy a stunning view of the town and its surrounds. Malcolm Saville, author of the *Lone Pine* books, who had a strong Christian faith, was interviewed for the *Songs Of Praise* programme that came from the church in 1977.

Having turned right just before reaching the church door, you proceed along a passage, now back on Church Square, and continue to the junction with West Street at the north-west corner of Church Square. The Old Vicarage, on the right of the passage, was the home of the Padre in the *Mapp & Lucia* books. Go forward onto West Street, noting to your left the Old Customs House (E. F. Benson's Poppits), and then swinging right. Almost immediately after the right bend you will meet Lamb House on your left. Mike Peters (in his book *Sussex Literary Lives*) describes Lamb House, an early eighteenth-century red-brick building and a classic piece of Georgian architecture, as possessing 'an aura of quiet and dignified detachment'. It has been the sometime home or lodging of a number of distinguished twentieth-century writers including the biographer Montgomery Hyde, the children's author Rumer Godden, and the publisher Sir Brian Batsford. It is best known, however, for its association with the novelists Henry James and E. F. Benson.

Henry James was born in New York in 1843 and established a reputation as an essayist and reviewer in the 1860s, with his first novel, *Watch and Ward*, published in 1871. He settled in England in 1876 and lived in London for the next 20 years, writing several novels including *The Europeans*, *Daisy Miller*, *Portrait of A Lady*, and *Washington Square*. Whilst based in London he also wrote short stories, essays, critical studies, travel works and drawing room comedies. In 1896, he rented Point Hill in Playden, just outside Rye, moving to the Old Rectory later that year and buying Lamb House in 1898, describing it as 'the very calmest and yet cheerfulest that I could have dreamed'. After making various improvements to the house, he lived there until his death in 1916, penning some of his finest novels there, including *The Wings Of A Dove* in 1902, *The Ambassadors* in 1903, and *The Golden Bowl* in 1904. During his time at Lamb House he was visited by some of the most notable writers of the time, such as H. G. Wells, Rudyard Kipling, G. K. Chesterton, Hilaire Belloc, Joseph Conrad, Ford Madox Ford and Sir Edmund Gosse. Patric Dickinson writes warmly of him, despite his being technically an incomer: 'And what came up was exotic and yet native, An American – almost Ryer, a curious equation, but he was.'

After Henry James' death, Lamb House was taken by E. F. Benson, who in his *Mapp & Lucia* books called it Mallards. Little Sussex House, a little further down West Street and on the other side, was the home of the fictitious Captain Puffin, with the imaginary Major Flint living opposite. The described walk shortly turns left into Mermaid Street, but by detouring down West Street you will see Santa Maria on the left, Hopkins' Fishmonger of the *Mapp & Lucia* books, with The Other House a little beyond becoming Benson's fictional fruiterer.

But back to the books' creator. Edward Frederic Benson was born in 1867 at Wellington College, Berkshire, and was educated at Marlborough and King's College, Cambridge. He wrote over ninety books, which included a number of comic novels about Dodo between 1914 and 1921 and, of course, Lucia, writing *Queen Lucia* in 1920 and *Lucia In London* in 1927. The *Lucia* books sprang to fame in 1985 with their dramatisation on television starring Prunella Scales and Nigel Hawthorne. Additionally, between 1911 and 1940, the year of his death, Benson published five autobiographical volumes. He has been described as Rye's most famous and best-loved author, and certainly he has set more of his bestselling books in Rye (albeit fictionalised as Tilling) than any other author on this literary pilgrimage. Indeed, many locals say they can still recognise some of the characters from the books, and during the summer visitors may take a guided walk round E. F. Benson's Rye. There is a 'Tilling Map' available in Rye, showing the probable locations of the inhabitants of the novels, published by the Tilling Society, the official E. F. Benson Appreciation Society. The map prudently warns the literary tourist that most of the houses are now private, so you have no excuse for wandering into an unsuspecting Rye-dweller's front room claiming to be looking for Hopkins' Fishmonger or Captain Puffin.

Beyond Lamb House, turn left into Mermaid Street. This steeply cobbled street has little sympathy for wheelchair or pushchair users (I write from experience!) but if you are not

Benson-ed out, you may wish to know that this was Porpoise Street of the *Mapp & Lucia* books, with the first house on the left being a dentist's surgery and Hartshorn House further down on the right-hand side being Wyses.

The Mermaid Inn is arguably the most eye-catching building on the street. It was bought in 1913 by the mother of the writer Richard Aldington who, as a result of his wartime experiences, produced his powerful anti-war novel *Death Of A Hero* in 1929. Marguerite Radclyffe Hall spent some time lodging at The Mermaid whilst waiting for The Black Boy in the High Street to be ready.

On the other side of the road the fine Jeake's House was, during the Depression years, the home of Conrad Aiken, an American poet, short-story writer and novelist. Aiken was born in 1889 and died in 1973; his fiction and his poetry reflected his interest in psychology, and he was much influenced by the work of Sigmund Freud and the author Edgar Allan Poe. During his time in Rye, Aiken was visited by the novelist Malcolm Lowry, best known for his 1947 novel *Under The Volcano*; his first novel, *Ultramarine*, having appeared in 1933. Aiken was not only a prolific writer, but a talented one: his *Selected Poems*, published in 1929, won the Pulitzer Prize, He continued writing for almost forty years thereafter, and in 1967 he published a book-length poem with one of the shortest titles you could imagine: it was simply called *Thee*.

Your literary pilgrimage is now drawing to an end. It only remains for you to descend to the foot of Mermaid Street and turn right into The Mint, which bends round to the right and becomes the High Street, and in due course you will arrive back at the Martello Bookshop which is on the left. If you need a final fix of *Mapp & Lucia* locations, you could detour left down Market Road, just beyond the junction between High Street and West Street, and go to the T-junction at the end; the house on the left corner at the T-junction rejoiced in the splendid Bensonian name of Woolgar and Pipstow. Returning up Market Street (Malleson Street in the stories), a house about halfway up on the left was the location of Benson's character Dr Dobbie.

Returning to the Martello Bookshop, you will be well supplied with copies, or information on where to find copies, of works by most, if not all, of the authors referred to in this walk, and if you want to extend the literary theme to your well-earned refreshment, there's always Fletcher's House up by the church. If you have any more time to spare in Rye, you may feel inspired to use this lovely town as a basis for penning the opening words of your own immortal poetry and prose. Failing that, there's always Woolworths ...

Chapter Seven

Best Ghost Walk

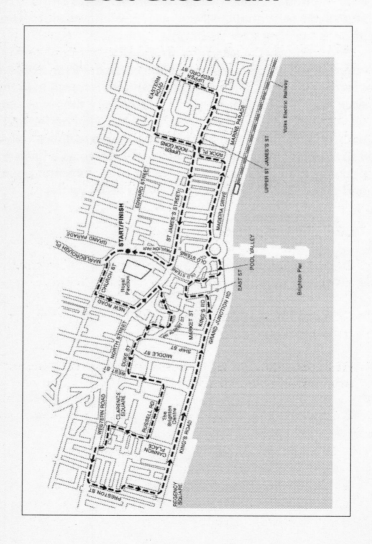

ACCESS BY CAR: You can approach Brighton from the A23 from the north, the A270 from Shoreham, or the A259 from Hove.

PUBLIC TRANSPORT: Brighton is served by frequent trains from Lewes, London, Chichester and Worthing.

START AND FINISH: Royal Pavilion, Old Steine, Brighton.

LENGTH: Approximately 3 miles.

DURATION: Anything from an hour to a day, as there is so much to see in Brighton.

CONDITIONS: Very easy – street walking throughout.

REFRESHMENTS: There are numerous pubs and cafés in Brighton.

The problem with a ghost walk is that ghosts are capricious creatures and cannot appear to order. However, Brighton has had more than its fair share of ghostly sightings and sounds in recent years, and even if you are unfortunate (or fortunate) enough not to meet a ghost on your journey through, you can at least enjoy a fascinating walk past some of the principal attractions of this bustling resort. Who knows, you may strike lucky when you least expect to ...

Brighton as it is today only really began to develop during the latter part of the eighteenth century; previously it was little more than a herring fishing community. The man indirectly responsible for putting Brighton on the map was Dr Richard Russell who, in 1750, was practising as a doctor in Lewes and sent patients to Brighton to try a seawater cure. He was one of several promoters of health who encouraged people to visit Brighton. Perhaps the most colourful entrepreneur in this field was an Indian, Sake Deen Mahomed, who established Mahomed's Warm, Cold and Vapour Baths. Arising from this concern for health, a number of famous people were drawn to Brighton towards the end of the eighteenth century, including Fanny Burney and Dr Johnson. In 1765 the Duke of Gloucester arrived, to be followed in September 1783 by his nephew, the Prince of Wales, later the Prince Regent and King George IV; the royal doctor had apparently recommended sea bathing as a remedy for his swollen neck glands.

The influx of the wealthy to Brighton sparked off a veritable explosion of building in the town, with many examples of splendid Regency architecture remaining very much evidence today, such as Hanover Crescent, Montpellier Crescent, Belgrave Place, Powis Square, Bedford Square, Regency Square, Russell Square and Clifton Terrace. Two of the most notable buildings constructed in Brighton during the nineteenth century include the Grand Hotel, designed in Italian Renaissance style and regarded as the leading hotel of its day in 1864, and St Bartholomew's Church, then the biggest brick church in Europe, magnificently decorated with oil paintings and Italian mosaics.

The first pier to be erected in Brighton was the Suspension Chain Pier, constructed in 1823, although it was destroyed by a storm in 1896. The currently derelict and disintegrating West Pier followed in 1866 and the still flourishing Palace Pier in 1899. Now designated as a city (with Hove), Brighton is certainly the most cosmopolitan place in Sussex, and has been dubbed 'London by the Sea'. If you fancy a meal in Brighton you can sample an amazing variety of exotic foods, and for a comfortable night's sleep, the Presidential Suite in the Grand Hotel was yours (in 2001) for £1,350 a night. Brighton is also a shopaholic's paradise; besides the usual chain stores, you will find some 700 independent shops offering everything from kinky boots to fetish chocolate cake.

But Brighton does have its darker side. Its growth in popularity as a resort, helped enormously by the arrival of the railway in 1841, produced its own social problems and tensions. It is perhaps not surprising that many restless souls, perhaps as a result of their tragic or untimely deaths, continue to create chaos and mayhem among the contemporary populace in such diverse places as department store basements and BBC broadcasting offices.

With a due sense of fear and trepidation you begin your walk at the Royal Pavilion on the corner of Marlborough Place and Church Street. In 1815 the Prince Regent appointed John Nash to build a palace to effectively replace the simple Marine Pavilion by Henry Holland, and the Royal Pavilion was the result. It was completed in 1823 and remains the most stunning building in Brighton, both inside and outside, the most notable rooms being the Music Room, the Great Kitchen and the Banqueting Room. It has seen a number of hauntings. Between the World Wars, on the occasion of a banquet, a caterer inspecting the table settings saw an elderly rotund woman coming from the kitchen wearing a long bunched-up skirt, triangular shawl and large bonnet. She was thought to be the ghost of Martha Gunn, the so-called 'bathing lady' who was one of the early promoters of health in the footsteps of Dr Russell. Other ghosts here include a male who said 'Thank you! Thank you!' to a lady making a bed, but who disappeared as she looked round; a frightened man in drab clothing who appeared to a security officer in 1991; and a man dressed in a shirt of silvery satin with cream pantaloons who was seen to climb an invisible staircase in 1993. In the spring of 1993, students saw the cowled figure of a ghostly monk in the Pavilion grounds.

In the Dome, immediately adjacent to the Pavilion, there have been a number of sightings of the White Lady, a woman in a long white dress resembling the morganatic wife of George IV, Maria Fitzherbert. A security officer reports seeing a portly man with cream pantaloons and leather riding boots, at least seven feet tall.

Turn left off Marlborough Place to head up Church Street. Opposite are the offices of BBC Southern Counties Radio, formerly the Blenheim, where a young chambermaid committed suicide. Numerous bizarre and unexplained incidents have been reported here, such as sensations of cold in various parts of the building; a piece of paper in a typewriter flipping backwards and forwards; a large cardboard box shooting off a filing cabinet and falling to the ground with a crash, but being found to be empty; coffee shooting out from a mug and splattering some records; tapes tumbling to the floor; broadcasting equipment and lights malfunctioning; and a mysterious smell of perfume.

Turn left off Church Street into New Road. On the corner of these streets is a building which, as the Mash Tun, has been haunted by a former landlady, Martha Boxell, who ran the pub here during the First World War. Subsequent owners have spoken of a feeling of being watched, and hearing the sound of footsteps; around 1992 or 1993 a lamp bulb is reported to have shot out of its socket, and a wall lamp to have shot into the air from its fitting and smashed on the floor.

Further down New Road is the Theatre Royal on the right, most famously haunted by the Grey Lady, so-called because of her old-fashioned grey dress. She has been seen in the vicinity of No 1 Dressing Room by two former staff members, and elsewhere in the building by lighting technicians, and she once tapped the actor Martin Jarvis on the shoulder. In 1982 she was seen by the actor Gerald Flood's wife, Anne, who heard a door banging and, on opening it, saw the Grey Lady for about a minute. Next to the Theatre Royal there used to be a restaurant called Il Teatro where, in October 1979, it was reported that a knife mysteriously flew through the air, narrowly missing the manager's daughter.

Follow New Road to the end, arriving at North Street. Cross North Street and turn left, continuing to its junction with Market Street. On the corner of these two streets are the buildings of the now defunct department store Hanningtons, where, in 1990, a Grey Lady (the Theatre Royal's Grey Lady or another?) was seen wearing a Victorian-style grey dress. In the mid-1970s there were reports of a mannequin in a long, silvery-grey dress appearing from nowhere, and there are also accounts of pressure to the shoulder and one of the lifts moving of its own accord.

Walk up Market Street, on which is the Druid's Head, a former fisherman's inn. Derek Woods, who took over the licence in 1975, says that in 1978 he saw a hooded figure, like a monk or a nun, flitting under the stairway in the main bar.

Continue up Market Street to a meeting of streets, aiming for the Opposition Café. You have now reached the Lanes. Long before the impact of Dr Russell, those who did not depend on the sea for their livelihood had their homes on higher ground in a labyrinth of medieval streets, and it is this higher ground that the Lanes occupy today. The original buildings have gone, and the current ones date mainly from the nineteenth century, but they give a good idea of the atmosphere of the medieval town, and provide an oasis of antiquity in this very bustling resort.

Pass the café and proceed up Nile Street, turning hard right into Meeting House Lane, arguably the most haunted street in Brighton. In this lane there was once a curio shop, which, in the 1950s, acquired a mysterious scent of fresh flowers of an unusually delicate bloom. It is said that a young man who worked in a florist's would bring flowers to his mother who worked here. When he announced his engagement to a local girl, the news so displeased his boss that he strangled him. The young man himself has been seen in the shop; he wears a sports jacket, is blessed with a head of fair hair, and has a favourite chair in which he sits.

A Free Church used to stand on the corner of Meeting House Lane and Union Street, which was converted into a pub called the Font & Firkin. During the conversion, work tools had a habit of moving themselves from one place to another, and in 1995 a barmaid saw a ghostly woman with a grey shawl over her head. Opposite the pub in Selby's Jewellers there have been reports as recently as the mid-90s of mysterious falling of plates from their wall fittings, the shattering of a glass door, and an exploding bottle of Coca-Cola.

Also in Meeting House Lane is the Bath Arms, once known as the True Briton. A former landlord is said to have drowned himself; was it he who has been seen in the bar wearing a tricorn hat, or on another occasion was leaning against a support pillar? And was it he who, in 1963, was responsible for an empty pint glass shooting several feet off a shelf and smashing?

The most famous ghost to be associated with the Lanes is a young nun whose punishment for elopement with a soldier was death by slow starvation. During the Second World War a woman on firewatch patrol in Meeting House Lane saw a spectre in a grey habit, and the nun reappeared in 1974. Also in Meeting House Lane, a middle-aged man was seen walking across the gallery of a teddy bear shop wearing a dark, knee-length top coat, while a customer who was visiting part of the shop in 1997 saw a pale-faced, scruffily-dressed little girl, aged about two, who sat on the stairs and then just faded away ...

Turn left off Meeting House Lane into Union Street, turn right into Ship Street and then left into Duke Street, ascending up Duke Street – a popular but expensive shopping area – to the end. Turn left into West Street, crossing this road. Two premises in West Street have ghostly pasts: witnesses at the Shark Bar, formerly Nellie Peck, have seen a vase shoot into the centre of the room, a spotlight dim and door slam of its own accord, while the Walkabout, formerly the New Regent, has a playful spirit that has caused items of clothing to vanish and cellar lights to extinguish automatically. A baby was heard calling 'mummy, mummy', even though no baby was present, and a man was seen with a chequered shirt, with his face and clothing covered in tiny, silver moving dots.

Pass the historic St Paul's Church and turn right into Russell Road. Follow it to its end, turning right into Cannon Place, going up this road until you reach Russell Square on the left. This is a most pleasant area, with attractive houses of varying colours and styles grouped round a nice garden. In the Regency Tavern here, a number of poltergeist incidents occurred some years ago, with moving furniture, swinging glasses and malfunctioning electrical equipment; recently a tall and 'rather wispy' woman was seen to walk straight through a temporary employee.

Return to Cannon Place and follow it to its end, turning left into Clarence Square. By turning right, you will immediately arrive at Churchill Square, Brighton's monumentally large shopping complex. Go left, westwards, along Clarence Square, turning right into Clarence Gardens; note the beautifully-kept little gardens and flower arrangements of the properties at the south end of Clarence Gardens. Then turn left into Western Road, the main street linking Brighton with Hove, and full of interesting shops. Pass Castle Street and turn left down Preston Street, taking the fourth left turn into Regency Square.

This is one of the most impressive areas of the city architecturally, with so many fine buildings (though it has to be said, some of them could do with a lick of paint). Staff of the Regency Hotel here report seeing an old woman, possibly a former landlady of a lodging house on the same site, in the Regency Suite, and occupants of the suite have spoken of a young woman who rushes towards a window and vanishes. It is believed she was a cripple who was afraid of gas lighting and jumped through the window to her death, leaving her clogs behind!

Proceed from here down to the seafront, passing the Royal Sussex Regiment memorial statue, and turn left into King's Road. You soon pass the massive Hilton, where a waitress preparing a table in the Cameo Room saw a tablecloth and its contents shoot about ten feet into the air and crash to the ground. Babies have been heard to cry here even though none were present.

Continue along Kings Road past the magnificent Grand Hotel and, beyond the end of West Street, the Town Hall; several people here claim to have seen the ghost of a monk expelled from St Bartholomew's Priory, and another ghostly sighting here is of a woman in a voluminous black dress, white pinafore and black conical hat. It is thought she may have been a matron in a workhouse that stood nearby.

Shortly beyond the Town Hall, turn left up East Street, another good shopping area. Around 1765, a fisherman by the name of Jervoise was arriving in the town with a catch of herring, when he saw dazzling shafts of light from the Rising Sun inn at the south end of this street. He banged on the door and the massive form of a ghostly man nicknamed Old Strike-a-Light appeared in front of him. Jervoise went into the inn to recover, only for the ghost to come and stand a few feet behind him. Jervoise slumped to the floor in a faint, and never regained consciousness.

In 1979, staff in what is now Sussex Stationers in East Street saw a spectre clad in a hooded robe, while occupants of the Greyhound in East Street experienced full gas cylinders being exchanged for empty ones, and their video player fast forwarding or ejecting cassettes without being invited. These ghosts have no consideration ...

Turn right out of East Street and immediately right again into Steine Lane, going forward to Pool Valley and coming out on the seafront. Turn left and you will find yourself at Brighton Pier (previously known as the Palace Pier). The Royal Albion Hotel opposite the pier, which was burnt down a few years back, is believed to be haunted with the ghost of one of Brighton's greatest impresarios, Sir Harry Preston. An engineer working here reports receiving a severe blow in one of the hotel bedrooms, and parts of the hotel have been found to be unusually cold for no obvious reason.

Proceed eastwards along Marine Parade (the A259 Newhaven road), following the landward side but still enjoying fine sea views. Just beyond the New Steine turning you turn left up Rock Place. In the Battle of Waterloo pub in this road there was once an apparition of a woman in a long grey dress, and also a ghostly coachman who in the 1970s was seen walking towards the gents and who in 1996 was said to glide through the front door. It is believed that the nineteenth-century coachman was driving the mayor and his daughter to an evening function, and a highwayman held up the coach and killed both the mayor and the coachman.

Turn right from Rock Place into St James Street, going forward into Upper St James Street. You are now in the Kemp Town area of Brighton, one of the more bohemian areas of the city with an atmosphere all its own. At the end of Upper St James Street, just before it becomes Bristol Road, turn left into Upper Bedford Street. Along this street, the Stag Inn has a resident ghost named Albert, a former landlord resplendent in large apron and black bands round each arm, who has been known to disconnect the keg beer gaslines. It is suggested that this is because he disapproves of the keg beer and prefers real ale!

At the end of Upper Bedford Street, turn left into Eastern Road and follow this westwards, shortly turning left into Upper Rock Gardens. Near the junction of this road and Edward Street (the continuation of Eastern Road) was a junk shop. In about 1970 its owner received a visit from a Mr McColl, a secondhand book dealer, who was granted permission to browse round the shop later in the owner's absence. While browsing, he was conscious of being watched, and felt an icy chill. Looking towards an archway, he saw a cloud that turned itself into the shape of a woman, but her features resembled those of a hideous corpse. Mr McColl flung a book at her, only for it to go right through her and hit the wall beyond. It was discovered that sixty years previously a woman had been murdered here by her husband, and her dismembered body had simply been dumped.

Proceed, with some relief, away down Upper Rock Gardens to its junction with St James Street, then turn right to follow this street down to Old Steine. Cross to the far side of Old Steine, and turn right up the road to reach the Royal Pavilion. Your walk is complete, although there are many more stories of ghostly apparitions in Brighton and its surrounds. But even if you have seen no ghosts, you will still have seen the best of Brighton – and if on your bus journey back to the station a light bulb suddenly flies from its fitting, or you feel a non-existent hand resting on your shoulder, don't be alarmed. It was only the man who died of boredom waiting for the 6B bus back to Worthing.

Chapter Eight

Best Pub Walk

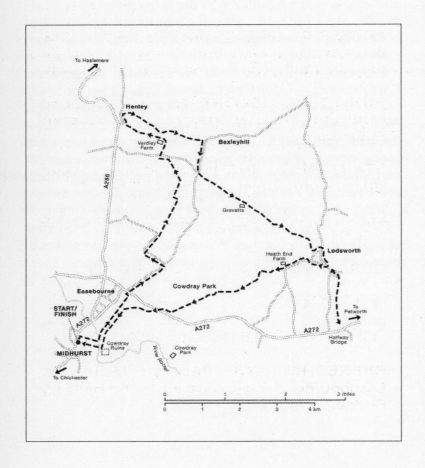

ACCESS BY CAR: Midhurst is on the A286 between Haslemere and Chichester and on the A272 between Petersfield and Petworth.

PUBLIC TRANSPORT: Regular buses to Midhurst from Haslemere, Chichester, Pulborough and Petworth.

START AND FINISH: Tourist Information Office, North Street, Midhurst.

LENGTH: 10 miles – can be extended by 1.5 miles.

DURATION: Roughly 4 hours' walking.

CONDITIONS: Easy walking along clear paths, tracks and minor roads with just one stiff climb. A fine day is essential.

REFRESHMENTS: Pubs at Midhurst, Easebourne, Henley, Lodsworth and Halfway Bridge.

Walkers in Sussex are spoilt for choice when it comes to a good country pub. After a bracing walk on the Sussex Downs there are few things more pleasurable than a homecooked pub meal with a glass of real ale or local cider. This walk will take you through some of the loveliest and most unspoilt scenery in Sussex, including some excellent woodland and parkland and incorporating glorious views to the surrounding downland, and will visit three deliciously quaint villages and a historic country town. Thirsts before, during and after the walk will be quenched and appetites satisfied by a string of pubs that have been acclaimed locally as well as nationally for their fine food and beer. Moreover, the walk has tremendous flexibility with many possibilities for shortening it or even bussing part of it to enable you to be at the pub of your choice at the time food is available.

If you wanted to do justice to all the pubs described, you could consider breaking the walk into two days. On the first day you might make a leisurely start from Midhurst, enjoying a mid-morning tipple in Easebourne, lunching in Henley and then taking the bus back to Midhurst for an evening's pubbing. On day two you could catch the bus to Henley, walk to Lodsworth and then enjoy lunch at Lodsworth or Halfway Bridge, going forward to Midhurst on foot. Or you could start the walk at Lodsworth, stopping at Midhurst or Easebourne for elevenses, lunching at Henley and returning to Lodsworth for an evening meal. Of course, you may decide that Midhurst has so many good pubs you won't want to leave the town at all!

Midhurst is a delightful old town; its focal point is North Street with its Georgian buildings and the fine Angel Hotel which, although refaced in the nineteenth century, is considerably older than that. The original town centre is away from the shopping area and is to be found around the Market Square, reachable from North Street via Knockhundred Row. It has many good half-timbered and Georgian houses; one of the most impressive buildings is the Spread Eagle, an old coaching inn with a sign claiming the date of 1430.

Among other buildings of particular interest are the half-timbered and tile-hung seventeenth-century library, the sixteenth-century timbered Market Hall, the Old Market House, also half-timbered and of the sixteenth century, and the Church of St Mary Magdalene and St Denys, parts of which date back to the thirteenth century. There is a pleasantly old-fashioned feeling about its streets and the number of small family businesses; it's like going back 30 or 40 years.

Of the many pubs in Midhurst, two have been singled out for inclusion in national pub guides. The Wheatsheaf, on the main road and effectively at the top end of the main shopping street, is an attractive, relaxing, low-beamed and timbered sixteenth-century building, offering good value and generous food with a particularly good sandwich choice. Beers include Ballards Old Ale, and King and Barnes.

The Crown, in Edinburgh Square, is another sixteenth-century building and is particularly noteworthy for its choice of beers which include Fuller's London Pride, Cheriton Pots and up to 8 guest beers at any one time with up to 150 guests per year. Favoured guests are Cheriton, Hampshire, Ballards, Hogs Back, Tripple FFF, Oakham, Rooster's, Ringwood, Hop Back and Woodforde's. Beer festivals are occasionally held here as well, and the pub is open all day. Perhaps the question is not whether you will want to go out walking after a session here, but whether you will physically be able to ...

On leaving the tourist information office, turn right and immediately right again onto North Street, and almost at once you will see, on your right-hand side, a path heading straight for the Cowdray Ruins. Join this path and follow it, the town's main (free) car park just to your right, and at the end you meet a T-junction with a metalled drive. Turn left here, perhaps pausing to admire the magnificent ruins which are directly opposite you as you reach the junction.

It was the then owner of the Cowdray Estate, Sir David Owen, who began building a grand country house in High Tudor tradition on the estate at the start of the sixteenth century. The project was completed by Sir Anthony Browne, Henry VIII's Master of the Horse, during the reign of Queen Elizabeth, who was herself entertained here in 1591. The mansion was destroyed by fire in 1793, leaving behind the ruins you see today.

Having turned left, proceed along the drive, then when the drive bends to the left, don't bend with it but keep going in the same direction, the track now becoming rougher. You very shortly go over a crossroads of tracks, then continue along the track, climbing gently. To your right are the polo fields of the Cowdray Estate, and immediately alongside the track are simple wooden stables for the polo horses. Carry straight on along the track which levels out slightly and becomes a metalled road as it arrives at the A272. Turn left and you find yourself in Easebourne.

Easebourne is a most attractive village with several fine half-timbered houses and sandstone cottages, some belonging to the Cowdray Estate. It once boasted a thirteenth-century Augustinian priory, the buildings of which fell victim to the Dissolution, but long before that the nuns had scandalised the neighbourhood with their behaviour; the prioress is even alleged to have given birth. The church, on the main road, has some Norman features but is described in Pevsner's *Buildings of England* guide as having suffered a 'catastrophic restoration – almost everything is 1876 at its hardest and worst'. Easebourne, pronounced 'Ezbourne' incidentally, has two curiosities: a bypass bridge, intended to keep horse traffic off its busy main road, and a street with the bizarre name of Wheelbarrow Castle.

Follow the A272 briefly – take care, as it is a very busy road – then turn right into Easebourne Street and follow it uphill. Note the little bridges and stream running alongside the street, adding to the beauty of this village. You soon pass The Olde White Horse which is on the left-hand side of the road; it is a cosy pub, with fireside armchairs and offering Greene King IPA, Abbot and Old Speckled Hen. However, it is still a little early in the day for a stop. You may want to detour here on your way back instead! Continue up the hill, passing a school on the same side of the road as the pub, and a couple of hundred yards beyond the school you see a very narrow road going off to your left. You need to take this road. At the junction is a sign advertising parking for The Holly Tree pub which is just a little further up the road you are leaving here, so if you find yourself walking past the Holly Tree, you've gone too far. However, you may want to stop off at The Holly Tree, which is included in the *Quiet Pint* guide for those who prefer their pubs without piped music. Badger Best, Guinness and Carlsberg are all available free of accompanying muzak, and there is a good wine list and range of malt whiskeys. The pub also offers excellent food: lunchtime brings fresh salmon mayonnaise, curried prawns and rice, and whole grilled plaice, while in the evening you can enjoy roast Aylesbury duck and pan-fried trout fillets, which the landlord claims he catches himself!

Follow the very narrow road as stated above; this rises up quite steeply in the shade of trees and bends to the right almost at a right-angle, with tracks going off ahead and to the left at this point (effectively, it's a crossroads). Continue rising with the road, sunken beneath large tree-lined cuttings, until you reach a fork, with rough tracks going right and left. Here the comfort of metal ends. Take the right fork and follow what is at first quite a wide track but which soon becomes no more than a public path passing through fields. Looking back, you now have a magnificent view of the South Downs escarpment as well as the more level wooded countryside around Midhurst. With unspoilt woodland now immediately ahead of you, this is most pleasant walking.

The path enters the wood, and at once you arrive at a T-junction with a track. Turn left onto this track which soon swings to the right and goes over a wide crossing track. Look out, very shortly thereafter, for a signed path forking left. You take this path, which proceeds on through pleasant woodland, over another wide crossing track, and forward to reach a metalled road. Turn left onto this road, then very shortly right onto a track signposted for Verdley Farm. Follow the track past the farm buildings, and you will see a signpost directing you left. Observing the sign, you swing left to continue across a field, keeping the farm buildings to your left and aiming for a gate at the far end of the field. There are superb views from the field northwards to the beautiful countryside around Black Down, a wooded hill very close to the border with Surrey. Go through the gate and continue along the path on the other side, ignoring a left fork. The views remain excellent.

You lose height, fairly gently at first then rather more rapidly, and at one point there are a couple of steep steps to negotiate. You arrive at a metalled road, the traffic noise of the nearby A286 all too audible, and turn right to follow the road, which leads unerringly down to the village of Henley. It is pleasantly quiet compared with the A286, but watch for motorists who also have their sights set on the Duke of Cumberland pub; smug self-satisfaction that you've got there by your own honest toil won't count for much if you find yourself swept under the wheels of a four-door family hatchback.

Henley is a delightful little place, and although there are no buildings of great importance, the array of cottages on the hillside makes a picturesque sight indeed. Among the finest buildings in the village is the next pub on the walk, the Duke Of Cumberland, a stone-built cottage covered with wisteria. The pub has a large garden rich in vegetation including lilacs and willows, and there is a stream and a pond full of trout. From the garden there are beautiful views northwards to Black Down. There are two low-ceilinged rooms, with a log fire in each and gas lamps on white-painted panelled walls. Food on offer includes homemade soup, filled rolls, liver pâté, ploughmans and 'late breakfast'. It is a free house with a good range of beers on offer including Adnams Broadside, Ballards Best, Gales Bitter and HSB, Hop Back Summer or Winter Lightning tapped from the cask, and farm ciders. Note that the pub shuts between 3 p.m. and 6 p.m.

To continue, emerge from the pub and look for the phone box more or less opposite on the right-hand side of the road. There is a footpath sign here pointing down what looks like a driveway to residential properties; follow the driveway and very shortly, just past Yew Tree Cottage, turn left onto a footpath, as directed by the signpost. The going is initially narrow, and the path descends and swings right quite suddenly to cross a footbridge, but then proceeds more sedately and decisively in a roughly easterly direction through most pleasant woodland. Ignore crossing tracks and continue more or less in a straight line. Soon you emerge from the thicker woods, the path skirting the right-hand edge of these and now keeping much younger trees to the right, giving a more open walk. A signed path tempts you back into the thicker woods but ignore this, and stick to the path you are on, remaining on the fringes of the younger woodland, and climbing quite steeply. In muddy conditions this could be quite an arduous climb.

As the ground levels out, you will see Verdley Farm again to your right. Continue on through now thicker woodland to arrive at a T-junction with a metalled road. Turn right onto this, and follow it downhill for a few hundred yards. You meet a metalled road going off to the right and, immediately opposite, three paths going off to the left – effectively a three-pronged fork. There is a bridleway sign pointing at the fork, and the path you want is the middle one. You join and follow what is an excellent track, giving magnificent views to the South Downs escarpment to the right, while the woodland to the left is a most pleasant prospect as well. You soon arrive at the buildings marked on the map as Grevatts, with a fingerpost pointing left towards a stile. Turn left to cross the stile, then bear immediately right along a good track, with excellent views to your left. The scene is only slightly marred by a long line of pylons, although even these have a certain grandeur and dignity.

Pass under the pylons and continue, approaching the attractive buildings of Vinings to your right. As you get near to these buildings, you reach a T-junction of tracks. Turn left here and follow the track, ignoring turnings off to the right. The track descends gently to reach a T-junction with a road, now on the edge of Lodsworth; turn right onto this road, very soon reaching a road T-junction with Shepherds Lane. Turn left onto Shepherds Lane, then at the end turn right into Lodsworth's main street.

Lodsworth is a most attractive village with a good mixture of old and new; its finest buildings include the Manor House, parts of which date back to the thirteenth century, the eighteenth-century Great House, the early-eighteenth-century Dower House, and the Church of St Peter, with some Norman work and a tower that dates back to about 1300, as well as a fine new window with its portions of stained glass.

Proceed down the main street, soon reaching the Hollist Arms on your right. This pub has been described as 'one of the best kept secrets in West Sussex'. It dates back to the sixteenth century and has a warm ambience, with old beams, an open fireplace and pine tables, plus a spacious secluded garden at the rear. Real ales are served, and, being a free house, the pub can offer some old favourites alongside beers from the Horsham brewery, as well as some fine wines at reasonable prices. The real forte of the Hollist Arms is its food. The *Chichester Observer* wrote that 'the food is perfectly cooked, appealingly presented and servings are more than generous, offering excellent value for money and achieving standards well beyond normal pub food'. There will usually be five or six fish dishes available at dinner, all absolutely fresh, while other evening delights might include cream cheese and chives wrapped in smoked salmon or brie wedges wrapped in pastry as starters, with main courses including pan-fried pork steak with Calvados and onion sauce, whole baked bream, and Selsey crab salad. Lunches include sautéd chicken in lobster sauce and Hollist cobs filled with anything from pâté to prawns. Oh yes, and puddings ... Italian ice cream, pineapple cheesecake and a combination of soft chocolate mousse with layers of biscuit base known as Mud Crunch!

Pub connoisseurs really are spoilt for choice hereabouts, for barely a mile away is another great pub, The Halfway Bridge Inn. To get there, continue down the main street from the Hollist Arms as far as Tudor Cottage on the left. Turn left here into Church Lane. Go down the road to a junction with a metalled road; by the junction is the lychgate of the church. Turn right onto the metalled road, which soon becomes more of a track. As the track bends left, don't bend left with it, but go straight ahead onto a footpath which descends to reach a T-junction with a rather wider track. Turn right at the track and simply follow it onto the Halfway Bridge Inn, just a few hundred yards down.

The inn was built in 1710; it was a staging post on the road between Dover and Winchester, and consists, to quote the 2002 *Good Pub Guide*, of a 'charming sprawl of differently aged buildings'. The rooms contain real fires, with masses of dried hops adorning the walls and low ceilings. Lunchtime food represents excellent value, with open sandwiches and light lunchtime meals on offer; a particular house speciality is Cumberland sausage with grain mustard mash and onion gravy. Beers include Gales HSB, Fuller's London Pride and Cheriton Pots Ale, while guest bitters include Becketts Old Town Bitter, Harveys Old, and Charles Wells Bombardier. There are usually two guests on offer at any one time, changed each week, making approximately 100 guests per annum. If you aren't a beer drinker, you may prefer to enjoy the locally produced Gospel Green cider. Note that the pub is shut between 3 p.m. and 6 p.m.

To get back to the course of the circular walk, simply retrace your steps to the Hollist Arms, remembering to fork left onto the narrower footpath where the bridleway sign points you straight on. A touch of the hair of the dog at the Hollist Arms may provide you with the necessary zest for the final stretch if you feel worn out by the extra mileage – or indeed by the Cumberland sausage.

Turn off the main street at the Hollist Arms (a left turn if you have approached it from Halfway Bridge, a right turn if you've missed it out) and follow the road signposted 'Recreation

Hall'. Continue along the road past the hall, ignoring the right turn into School Lane. At Heath End Farm the road bends left. Don't bend left with it but go straight on along the path, through the trees. You soon reach a T-junction of paths. Turn left then almost immediately right onto a signed path and follow it along the right-hand edge of a field, swinging left at the far right corner to follow the field edge beside woodland.

Towards the end of the wood, look for a path sign pointing right. Follow it, going up to the stile, and now look across an area of parkland, with fine views to the South Downs beyond. The course of the path is not distinct through the field beyond the stile, but take a roughly diagonal course. The ground rises slightly and as you reach the top of the rise you can look down to a pond, marked on maps as Stewards Pond. Aim for the left-hand edge of the pond and, having skirted its edge, aim for a gate straight ahead at the end of the field. Go through the gate and immediately turn right onto a good track which you follow uphill; as it gets more wooded, look for a left fork with footpath sign. Take this left fork and go uphill, crossing a fairway on the Cowdray Park Golf Course, aiming for a footpath sign on the other side and keeping in the same direction.

Signposting points you, with no real change of direction, clearly past the fifteenth tee and then past the left-hand side of the eighth tee. It looks rather private, but the right of way across the course is clear and you should not let golfers persuade you otherwise – although it might be trying their patience a little to plonk yourself down in front of the tee with a view to finishing off the Hollist Cob that you couldn't manage earlier.

Proceed now down the left-hand side of the eighth fairway. Providing you keep a wary eye out for maverick golf balls, this is lovely walking in quite charming surroundings – a pleasant place indeed for a game of golf. Roughly two thirds of the way down the fairway you will notice a green – the ninth green – to your left. Follow round the back of the ninth green but don't be tempted to continue straight on along the track; instead turn right to follow beside the ninth hole back to the ninth tee, and then follow an obvious path forward to meet the main road. This is the A272 you last saw at Easebourne or at Halfway Bridge if you made the detour. Don't cross the A272 yet, but turn right to walk briefly along the grass beside it, observing more of the golf course to your right and splendid views across the road to your left.

The clubhouse of Cowdray Park Golf Course soon comes into view, and as it does so, look for a gate and footpath sign across the road. You go over the road, taking great care, and now follow an excellent path downhill, heading for the polo fields. On summer weekends you may well see polo in progress and the surrounding area will be crowded with spectators as well as players.

At the bottom of the hill you reach a stile which you cross, then continue across grass in the same direction – wheels ruts mark the course of the right of way – until you reach the bottom right-hand end (as you look at it) of the polo field. Follow alongside the field, keeping the fence to your left, then shortly use a stile to cross into the field and proceed along the field edge in the same direction, the fence now on your right. This is really nice walking, the South Downs escarpment looking particularly impressive from here.

Stay with the fence, which now goes round to the right, and you soon arrive at the track that you were on earlier, linking Cowdray Ruins with Easebourne. Turn left and proceed past the stables downhill, going over the crossroads of tracks and forward onto the metal driveway leading you to the ruins. Turn right here on a signed path that brings you back to North Street in Midhurst. Now you need to decide where to pub away the evening – assuming any landlord will tolerate your own particular brand of Mud Crunch that nestles on the soles of your boots.

D&J July 2006 + and Easter Sunday 2019, though we parked here ® instead of here ⚠

Chapter Nine

Best Sunday Afternoon Walk

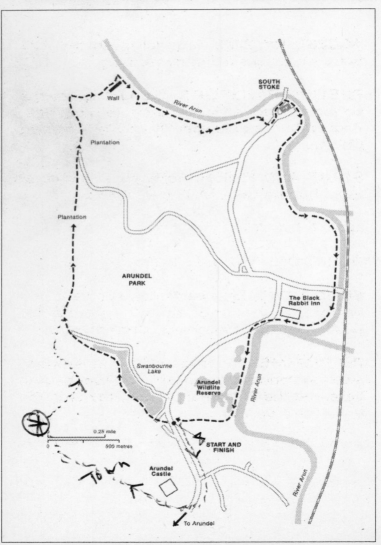

ACCESS BY CAR: Arundel is on the A27 between Chichester and Worthing.

PUBLIC TRANSPORT: Arundel is on the London Victoria–Portsmouth railway line. Regular buses to Arundel from Worthing and Chichester.

START AND FINISH: South-west corner of Swanbourne Lake, Mill Road, Arundel.

LENGTH: 5 miles.

DURATION: Two and a half hours.

CONDITIONS: Easy parkland, woodland and waterside walking, but unsuitable for pushchairs or wheelchairs. One stiff climb.

REFRESHMENTS: Huge choice in Arundel, also food and drink available at Swanbourne Lake and the Black Rabbit pub, towards the end of the walk.

Sunday afternoon can be an anticlimax. You may have enjoyed a good Sunday lunch, perhaps a roast with all the trimmings, but once the meal is cleared away, lethargy can easily creep in and before you know it, it's starting to get dark, and it's time to think about work on Monday. What better antidote to this post-prandial langour than a walk that certainly clears the cobwebs but is not excessively adventurous, starts and finishes in one of the most historic towns in Sussex with enough attractions to fill a day on its own, passes through a variety of landscapes, all of them very scenic, and will still get you home in time for the *Antiques Roadshow*.

At one time Arundel was an important port, and it was only in 1927 that the port finally closed. Arundel's chief glory is its castle, rebuilt in the eighteenth century and essentially a great country house that was built on the site of an earlier medieval fortress. It has been the seat of the Dukes of Norfolk and the Earls of Arundel for more than 700 years. It was severely damaged in the Civil War; all that remains of the original fortification are the twelfth-century shell keep and fragments of the thirteenth-century barbican and curtain wall. Today, the castle contains some furniture from the sixteenth century, some splendid tapestries and paintings by world-famous artists, and some heraldic artefacts from the Duke of Norfolk's collection.

Close to the castle, on London Road, is the town's Roman Catholic cathedral, commissioned by the Fifteenth Duke of Norfolk and built in Gothic style in the 1870s, although it was only designated a cathedral in 1965. Opposite the cathedral is the fourteenth-century St Nicholas Church, divided into separate Catholic and Anglican areas by a screen. The Catholic chapel within the church is known as the Fitzalan Chapel, where former Earls of Arundel and Dukes of Norfolk lie buried. Like the castle, it was very badly damaged in the Civil War but was restored in 1886, and boasts a magnificent east window as well as hugely elaborate stone canopies that top the tombs of the Arundels.

Both the High Street and Tarrant Street, leading off it to the right, house large numbers of cafés, pubs, restaurants, antique and gift shops, and specialist stores selling everything from books to bric-a-brac, fudge to furniture, and watercolours to walking boots (Peglers, the outdoor specialists, has several shops in Arundel). Sunday trade is particularly brisk. Tourists aren't necessarily welcomed everywhere with open arms – literally: one tearoom enforces a strict policy of not admitting any gentleman without a sleeved shirt!

To start your walk, and on the basis that you have explored Arundel first, you'll need to make your way from the High Street onto the river bridge (you can't miss it). Immediately before the bridge, turn left into Mill Road and follow it past the bowling green, tennis courts and putting green, enjoying superb views across the Arun Valley to your right and the castle to your left. You come to a humpbacked bridge over a little tributary of the Arun. Cross the bridge and shortly beyond, you will see a signed footpath going away to your left. Take this path, which follows the west side of Swanbourne Lake, a very picturesque and very popular local amenity. Refreshments are available at Swanbourne Lodge, accessible by taking the next entrance to the lake off Mill Road. Please note that the lake area is closed to the public on 24 March each year.

You continue along the lakeside path, keeping the waters to your right, and at length arrive at the top end of the lake. There is a stile and signed path straight ahead, but ignore this first stile and swing right with the main path. Rather than swing right again to follow the lakeside path back towards Mill Road, climb a small embankment to reach a wide track just beside a gate and stile. Turn left, going over the stile, and follow the track, climbing slightly to reach a crossroads of tracks.

You are now in Arundel Park, an area of parkland of 1,000 acres; formerly a deer park, it is now used for sheep grazing, forestry and shooting. Bus travellers from Chichester, be warned: if you see a bus advertised to go to Arundel Park, make sure that it is Arundel where the bus is going, and not the Arundel Park in Chichester, which is a sprawling modern housing estate of considerably less aesthetic value.

At the crossroads of paths, turn right onto what seems an obvious and promising track, but almost immediately leave it by turning left onto a narrow path that goes very steeply uphill, aiming just to the right of an area of woodland. This is the steepest climb you'll have this afternoon, but all the better to work off your roast beef and Yorkshire pud. The path, after looking a little unpromising at first, now becomes rather more obvious, going forward to a stile, but beyond the stile, although a fingerpost points the way straight ahead, the path through the field is not at all clear. Aim for a pair of trees more or less straight ahead of you, and as you reach them you will see another fingerpost just to the right, again pointing reassuringly ahead. Follow the fingerpost to a clump of trees with a stile towards the left of them. Cross the stile and now, continuing in the same direction, aim for a footpath sign at the edge of the thick woodland that is directly ahead of you. All the while you have been gaining height and you can now reward yourself by looking back at a quite majestic view which includes Arundel Castle and the lowland countryside beyond, stretching to the sea which will also be visible on a clear day.

On reaching the footpath sign at the edge of the wood, turn left to follow a track which skirts this wood, and enjoy glorious views to the Arun Valley and the South Downs rising up behind. Beyond the wood the track bends left, but you continue in roughly the same direction along a signed path, again very indistinct, but use as your marker the left-hand end of a line of chalk cliffs you should see ahead of you. If you can't, you either had one glass of wine too many with your lunch and would be well advised to head home again while the going's good, or it's wet or misty, or possibly both, and therefore you won't have been so foolish as to have left the lunch table in the first place.

Using the left end of the cliffs to guide you, you should see a stile ahead of you at the edge of further woodland. Go down to the stile, cross it and now follow a much clearer path quite steeply downhill. This can be slippery after rain. You soon arrive at a T-junction of paths, turning right onto another well-defined track, but look out very shortly for a signed path going off to the left. This could easily be missed. You take this path and continue to descend, dropping down to a wall. You follow just to the left of the wall, parallel with it, until you reach a gate in the wall and here you turn right, through the gate. There is a Swanbourne signboard here. Immediately after going through the gate, turn right onto a track which will take you to the village of South Stoke. The path twists and turns through an area of woodland, climbs to emerge from the wood at a stile, proceeds along a field edge downhill, and swings right and then left into another wooded area. Signing is good and it is virtually impossible to go wrong.

Climb again and emerge, the track now wide and following another field-edge. The gaps in the trees to the left allow some good views to the Arun, although it is not easy to follow the course of the river because of the surrounding vegetation. This is truly rural, and the bustle of Arundel, though just three miles back, seems part of another world.

You now approach South Stoke, heralded by some farm buildings and a stern sign warning you to bear right beyond a flint wall. You do just that, the track proceeding parallel with the wall to a metalled road. Turn left onto the road, very soon reaching a left fork. Take this fork, which begins as a metalled road but soon becomes a track which passes by the church of St Leonard, South Stoke. The church dates from the eleventh century and boasts a tall, wide nave and chancel but no other Norman details. The tower, however, is medieval, and perched on it is what is quaintly known as a Victorian witch's hat spire.

Now the walking is very easy. Proceed on along the track to just short of a bridge over the Arun. Turn right onto the riverside path, keeping the river to your left. This is a tremendous walk along a good clear path, with the lovely Arun beside you and the South Downs rising up behind it, with Arundel Park to your right. Soon you will see Arundel Castle towering up above the trees.

After a mile or so the peaceful stroll is interrupted, if that is the right word, by the Black Rabbit pub, which used to be an alehouse for users of the now defunct Wey and Arun Canal. The path goes past the pub, the metalled courtyard actually part of your route. Leaving the pub buildings behind, you go forward to a road. Turn left onto the road, but very soon, just opposite the Coach House, turn left onto another riverside path.

In a little under half a mile you approach a gate, just before which is a path to the right, and you follow this path beside a narrow channel of water. To your right are the lakes and ponds of the Arundel Wildlife and Wetland Trust, with its fine collection of swans, ducks, geese and many migratory birds. The visitor centre and entrance is on Mill Road a short way beyond Swanbourne Lake. After a short, pleasant walk in the shade of trees you arrive at the humpbacked bridge on Mill Road. To return to Swanbourne Lake, turn right immediately before the bridge and climb the steps to rejoin the road, then right again to get back to the lake. To get to Arundel, turn left immediately before the bridge, and keep going. You've certainly walked off your Sunday lunch – hands up now for a pot of tea with scones, jam and clotted cream?

Chapter Ten

Best Church Walk

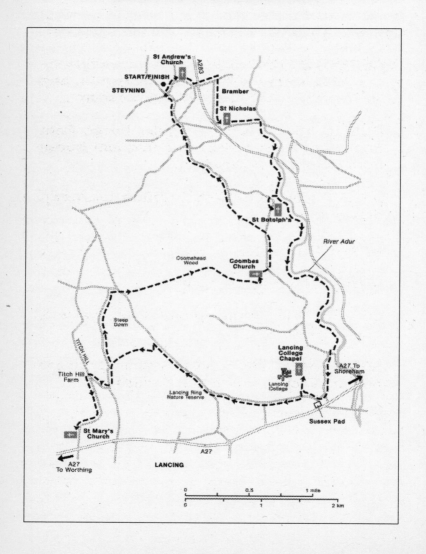

ACCESS BY CAR: Steyning is accessible via the A283 from the A24 at Washington, and via the A283 from the A27 at Shoreham.

PUBLIC TRANSPORT: Regular buses from Shoreham to Steyning, less frequent buses from Horsham to Steyning.

START AND FINISH: Truffles tearoom, Steyning.

LENGTH: 12 miles.

DURATION: Allow a full day.

CONDITIONS: Some up and down walking, but generally easy throughout.

REFRESHMENTS: Plenty at Steyning, just one pub at Lancing after about 5 miles.

Sussex has a tremendous variety of contrasting religious buildings, from the majesty of Chichester Cathedral to the ancient intimacy of Upmarden, from the architectural exuberance of St Bartholomews, Ann Street, Brighton, to the compact tranquillity of Lullington. Many beautiful churches lie on or close to the walks described elsewhere in this book. It might be thought strange that a 'best church walk' should be set in the somewhat unremarkable countryside between Steyning and Worthing. However, this countryside contains a number of historic churches that are very different in character, atmosphere and interest; there is no doubt at all that the surrounding scenery, though unspectacular, is most pleasant, with good hillside walking, great views, a long riverside stroll through one of the great river valleys of Sussex, and a beautiful town with which to start and end. In my view, it has pride of place among the church walks of Sussex, and will be of great interest and enjoyment even if you have no religious inclinations or vowed never to go near a church since your last visit when a funny old man in a white dress poured water all over you.

Steyning is a lovely base for your walk. This old town was founded in the eighth century by St Cuthman, an early Celtic Christian who travelled eastwards from Wessex pushing his mother in a handcart. The wheel on the cart broke when Cuthman arrived in the vicinity of what is now Steyning, causing the poor old lady to be thrown to the ground, a sight which provoked much cruel laughter from the nearby haymakers. By the late Saxon period had developed into an important port on the River Adur, which was then navigable. Silting of the river resulted in the harbour closing, but Steyning continued to thrive as a market town and boasts many historic buildings of flint, brick, timber, tile and thatch. Arguably its finest street is Church Street with many buildings of the fifteenth, sixteenth and seventeenth centuries, and ending in the particularly pleasant Chantry Green. Among Church Street's highlights, apart from the church (see below), are the Grammar School, built as the home of a religious order and retaining its fifteenth-century façade today; the Norfolk Arms, which was built as a private house in the seventeenth century; and the sixteenth-century timber-framed Saxon Cottage. Near the junction of Church Street with the High Street is a seventeenth-century house which has a central recess and overhanging wings. The High Street boasts the imposing tile-hung Old Market House, complete with projecting clock turret.

You begin at Truffles tearoom at Steyning; a tearoom is always a good place to begin a walk, especially with many miles ahead of you. Turn left out of the teashop and proceed down the main street, turning left into Church Street. Follow this, pausing every so often to view the fine old buildings of the street, until you reach St Andrew's Church, the first of six historic churches you will see on your day's walk, on the left-hand side. It is unmissable in every sense, and described by Simon Jenkins as a 'bruiser of a building'. The resting place of St Cuthman, it was given by Edward the Confessor to the Norman monks who demolished the Saxon church that previously stood here and built another church, of which a substantial part remains today. This includes the tremendous nave, chancel arch, and nave arcades and clerestories which had all been completed by the middle of the twelfth century. The arcades and clerestories are decorated with quite magnificent Norman carvings, described by Jenkins as a 'gallery of Norman art', depicting the heads of both humans and animals, and other features including stone zigzags, scallops and dogtooth.

In the sixteenth century there were two important additions

to the church: the west tower, which looks almost too small in comparison to the nave, and the reredos of 48 carved panels, one of which contains the coat of arms of Henry VIII. In the porch there is a broken coffin lid, taken from the Saxon burial ground; it is possible that it might have come from the grave of St Cuthman, or possibly that of King Alfred's father Ethelwulf.

Before you leave Church Street, see if you can spot a plaque outside a house proclaiming 'This is Sir Harry Gough's house, 1771'. The plaque was erected by the local MP following a difficult tenant's failure to pay the rent, believing that if he persisted the house would one day be his own!

You continue along Church Street, which becomes Cripps Lane. Continue along the lane, bending left to cross over the town's bypass, then turn right to follow the residential Roman Road. Go downhill along Roman Road, proceeding forward into the narrower Castle Lane, the noise of the traffic on the parallel bypass quite intrusive just here. Turn left at the end onto The Street to enter the village of Bramber. However, immediately upon reaching The Street, a path takes you off left to reach your second church, St Nicholas. It dates from the very first few years after the Norman Conquest and was built by William de Braose as part of the residences of the nearby Bramber Castle, and became effectively the castle chapel. Although the church lost its transepts and chancel in the Civil War, the Norman chancel arch remains, and there is some Norman carving around it, including what Keith Spence in *The Companion Guide To Kent And Sussex* describes as a 'very Chaucerian fox'! The church retains a tranquillity and simplicity that contrasts beautifully with the boldness of that of Steyning. Nearby is the ruin of the Norman castle, destroyed by the Parliamentarians in the Civil War;

all that is left is a 76-foot-high fragment of masonry on a steep hill.

Continue now eastwards along the right-hand side of the main street at Bramber, a pretty village with one of the finest timber-framed houses in Sussex: the fifteenth-century St Mary's House, built originally as a home for monks. Look out also for the amazing flowers bedecking Bramber Castle Hotel. Before the 1832 Reform Bill, Bramber was a classic 'rotten borough', returning two MPs for under a hundred inhabitants. One of the MPs was William Wilberforce, who campaigned against slave trading. It is said during his term of office he once went through the village quite unaware of its name!

Proceed eastwards along the main street until you reach the river bridge. Immediately before the bridge a path goes off to the right, descending to the banks of the River Adur. Follow this path. The prospect immediately ahead is not wonderful, with a busy road right in front of you, but having passed underneath it you find the surroundings become much pleasanter, with the South Downs both to your right and left.

Not far beyond the road bridge, a footbridge over the river can be seen ahead of you. Just before you get level with the footbridge, a path goes off to the right. This is the course of the South Downs Way, which features in a number of other walks in this book. You can take this path to detour to our third church, the church of St Botolph in the village of Botolphs. When you reach the road, simply turn left to arrive at the church, a comparatively small building but quite dignified in its own way, and towering proudly above the meadows beside the Adur. The exact date of the founding of the church is not known, but it is of Saxon origin and is believed to date back to about 950. The south wall of the nave and chancel arch and wall are Saxon, and date from the original construction. In the south wall of the nave there is one pre-Norman window and the headstone of another. Some traces of Saxon painting remain on the chancel arch; one figure that can be made out is that of an abbot, possibly St Botolph himself, but in years gone by the arch must have been a colourful sight indeed. The original north wall was removed in around 1250 when an aisle was added to accommodate the increasing population, and a little later the Saxon apse was replaced with the present chancel and the small tower was added. The only significant later addition to the church was the finely carved Jacobean pulpit and sounding board. On occasion, sermons were preached by the Archbishop of Canterbury, William Laud, whose efforts preserved the Church of England in Jacobean times and helped to suppress the excesses of Puritanism.

At the west end of the church stands the coat of arms of Charles II who passed through Botolphs on his flight to France and final exile. Today the church is a lovely, peaceful place where time really does seem to stand still. The village itself used to be a flourishing community and even had its own wharf, but the vagaries of the tides of the Adur caused the village to decline, and in 1534 the parish was legally wound up. Some pretty cottages remain, but the nearby cement works have undoubtedly blighted the surroundings and Pevsner puts it well when he sums up Botolphs as 'a tiny depopulated flint-built hamlet which has had the nineteenth and twentieth century thrown at it'.

Return to the riverbank the same way you came, and simply proceed along the west bank of the Adur. There is a tremendous contrast between the grimness of the scene across the river to the left – the cement works, the very busy A283 Steyning–Shoreham road, and a long row of terraced houses – and the beauty of the downland landscape to the right, as well as on the far side of the modern paraphernalia to the left. Once clear of the cement works, you should enjoy the riverside stroll, and make good fast progress along the obvious path.

Passing the works, you swing south-westwards, getting close to the hamlet of Coombes on your right, which you will see later in the day, then head sharply south-eastwards, before a further meander of the river again forces you south-westwards and then south-eastwards once more. The river then appreciably widens, and your path, having swung south-westwards again, then turns sharp left to follow a tributary channel.

Soon you arrive at a road – the same road, in fact, that you joined to reach the church at Botolphs. Turn left onto the road. (Note that the path shown on some maps as running from more or less straight across this road to The Drive, leading to Lancing College Chapel, has now gone.) There is then a tedious but unavoidable road walk to just before the junction with the A27. As you approach that junction, take the right-hand turn, which is the road to Lancing College. By then turning almost immediately left, you will arrive at the Sussex Pad, the only refreshment place on this walk. It also provides useful car parking. Local residents don't take kindly to your parking on the college approach road, as I discovered to my cost one stormy afternoon.

Don't continue down the college approach road, but more or less opposite the turn-off for the Sussex Pad you will see a footpath sign pointing north-westwards across the meadow. Pass through the gate to follow this path. It is a pleasant stroll through the meadow, bringing you back onto the college approach road but significantly nearer the college. Turn right and follow the road uphill, swinging left to continue onto the college, with the massive college chapel immediately to your right.

The chapel is visible for miles, and being right in the shade of it will make you feel very small indeed. Pevsner refers to its 'total romantic effect, a Gothic chapel as Turner might have imagined it in paint or Mendelssohn might have personified it in music'. It is open between 10 a.m. and 4 p.m. Mondays to Saturdays, and 12 noon to 4 p.m. on Sundays. As soon as you enter, you are immediately struck by its sheer vastness, the walls stretching heavenwards seemingly for ever. With an internal height of 94 feet it is the fourth highest church interior in England, being beaten only by Liverpool Cathedral, Westminster Abbey and York Minster; its external height, 150 feet, is impressive enough. At one time there were plans for a massive north tower, but it was never built.

Yet it is not a particularly historic building. Its foundation stone was laid in 1868, twenty years after the founding of Lancing College itself by Nathaniel Woodard, then curate at Shoreham, and to whom the chapel is a testament. It was built over a mixture of clay and flint, so the foundations had to be taken down 60 feet to the chalk. The style of the chapel is early-fourteenth-century English Gothic, with thirteenth-century French influences. Its outstanding features are its painted ceiling, the stunning stained glass Rose Window at the west end of the chapel, completed in 1978, and the magnificent tapestries above the High Altar, a miracle of painstaking handiwork, with their gilded figures and red backgrounds. They were designed by a Lady Chilston and woven at Merton Abbey in 1933; until the new tapestries at Coventry Cathedral were made, they were the biggest in England and are still among the largest in the world, measuring 35 feet high by 10 feet wide. Pevsner was less than kind about them, calling them 'hopelessly weak'.

BEST CHURCH WALK

It is unfortunately necessary now to retrace your steps, but the more arithmetically minded can at least enjoy working out how many churches of the size of the church of St Botolph could fit into Lancing College Chapel. Those of a less mathematical disposition will of course have a ready answer – a load of Botolphs.

Return the way you came, down the college approach road, but this time go past the junction with the path through the meadows, and continue past the Old Farm House on the right, and a small pond on your left. The road bends left and goes slightly uphill. As it bends, look for a track going off to the right, with a public footpath sign somewhat concealed by the surrounding foliage. Join this path. Shortly there is a left fork but don't be tempted – it just leads to a rubbish tip. Rise slightly, and enjoy an excellent view out to sea, the bustling town of Shoreham and its airport a short way away to your left. This path can be very muddy and slippery in wet weather, so do take care.

You soon arrive at a road; go straight on in the same direction up the road, in the shade of trees. The road degenerates into a stony track and you continue to follow it uphill, passing just to the right of Lancing Ring Nature Reserve. Ignoring paths leading off into the reserve, stick to the main track, which now climbs more purposefully, passing through a gate and continuing uphill. As you gain the crest of the hill, you pass through an attractive arch of trees.

The views hereabouts are absolutely superb. Looking back the way you came, you can see the massive conurbation of Brighton and Hove laid out before you, and on a clear day you will see as far as Seaford Head. To your left, as you walk, you will see the sea, and the large town of Worthing and its surrounds. To your right is the Adur Valley that you left behind not long ago, and although that ubiquitous cement works refuses to get out of the picture, it is somewhat dwarfed by the majestic downland scenery behind. I walked this section on a very unsettled but extraordinarily clear August afternoon with blue sky above me but huge pockets of menacing black cloud on every skyline, and the occasional rumble of thunder, the thrill of the stormy surroundings only just outweighing the fear that I might not get my daughter, plus pushchair, back to the car before one of the clouds emptied its contents all over us.

Having passed through the trees, you emerge into more open country with lovely downland scenery now ahead of you, and then begin to descend. You pass a fingerpost pointing the way ahead, and a little further downhill, you reach a second fingerpost indicating a path leading off left, with a stile very close by. The path is indistinct, but after just a few yards you arrive at a more clearly defined track, turning right onto it and proceeding north-westwards. To begin with you go roughly parallel with the wide track you just left, then swing in a more westerly direction and drop down to a crossroads of paths. Go straight over, keeping just to the right of an enclosure; you rise gently, then begin to descend steeply.

At the bottom you reach a line of pylons and a T-junction of paths. Turn left onto what is a wide track, follow it southwards, then in a few hundred yards turn right onto a track that goes north-westwards to meet the Sompting–Steyning minor road at Titch Hill Farm. Turn left onto the road. You now have a road walk for the best part of a mile, climbing initially then descending towards the busy and noisy A27 to arrive at St Mary's Church, Sompting, the fifth church of your walk.

St Mary's boasts England's finest Saxon steeple, built early in the eleventh century; the foundations can be traced back to 960! Each side of the tower ends in a steep gable, and the roof is made up of four diamond-shaped surfaces meeting in a point. It is known as Rhenish helm, and although it is common in the Rhineland in Germany, it is unique in England. The carvings on the arches of the tower interior, believed to date back as early as the steeple, are among the earliest examples of English architectural carving.

The church retains some splendid Saxon sculpture and carving: one clearly discernible figure is that of an abbot with a book propped up beside him, and other carvings include leaf scrolls with pomegranates in their centres. The rest of the church is mostly late Norman, dating from near the end of the twelfth century when the church was donated to the Knights Templar. They pulled down much of the original building, thankfully leaving the Saxon tower and carvings, and also a plain blocked early-twelfth-century doorway on the north side of the nave. A north transept and southern chamber were both added by the Knights Templar, the most privileged of knightly orders. In the early fourteenth century the Templars were suppressed and the church passed to another order, the Knights Hospitallers, who made further additions and returned the church to its original Saxon style.

Other things to look out for in the church are a thirteenth-century sculpture of Christ holding an open book, on the north wall of the nave, and the font, which has been in use since Norman times. Just east of the church is the flint and brick Sompting Abbots, now a school – the north transept of the church is the family chapel of the Crofts, sometime lords of the manor of Sompting Abbots with a number of memorials of the late eighteenth/early nineteenth centuries – but the village of Sompting itself is separated from the church by the A27. If you are desperate for some sustenance but want to avoid taking your life in your hands, you can always go down to the dual carriageway, turn right and walk for half a mile to the Sainsbury's superstore on the Lyons Farm Retail Park – which, shall we say, dates back slightly less far than the Sompting church steeple.

You now need to retrace your steps. Return by road to Titch Hill Farm, and then turn right to follow the track you took earlier. Follow this to a T-junction of tracks. Here, turn left up the track beside the pylons which you took earlier, but on reaching the next junction of paths do not take the right fork. Instead, carry straight on up the track northwards, climbing steadily. You pass below the Steep Down triangulation point, just under 500 feet above sea level, then swing slightly east of north, still gaining height, to arrive at a T-junction of paths. Turn right and follow a clear track eastward. Shortly the path swings right, but your way is straight ahead through a gate.

If you wish to detour to the triangulation point and viewpoint of Steep Down no more than a quarter of a mile away, do not go through the gate, but go a few yards past it and turn right onto a path that goes steeply uphill, the gradient moderating slightly as you get nearer the triangulation point. The views are breathtaking; on a clear day you can see Bognor Regis to the west, and the cliffs beyond Brighton to the east, while in the other direction there are excellent views to the Adur valley, and the South Downs and the Weald beyond it. You must then retrace your steps to continue.

Having passed through the gate, you continue along a reasonably well-defined path, a small patch of woodland immediately to your right, and shortly cross under a line of pylons. You now continue forward along what is a clear path which initially goes south of east then swings in a more easterly direction. This is superb walking, on a good straight path with a reassuring fence to your right and increasingly good views ahead to the Adur valley with which you will soon be reunited. The coastline, including the high-rise buildings of Brighton and the soaring walls of Lancing College Chapel, makes an impressive prospect to your right.

You aim unerringly for the little plantation marked on the map as Coombehead Wood. Before reaching the wood, however, you swing gently south-eastwards, still keeping the fence to your right. The path is not too well defined here, and you may well be tempted onto a clear stony track leading down the steep hillside immediately to your left, but don't take it; keep the fence immediately to your right, and soon a clearer path becomes apparent.

Now you descend very gently, enjoying lovely views ahead to the Adur Valley, but much closer at hand is the tiny community of Coombes, a group of houses and farm buildings that are separated from your hillside by an area of woodland. Continue alongside the fence until you get level with the wood. As you do so you approach a double gate, but immediately before this is a gate in the fence to your right. Pass through the gate in the fence and continue on very briefly in the same direction you have been following, the trees now very close on your left, and almost immediately on the left you'll see a signed footpath leading steeply down into the trees. You almost double-back on yourself, doing a sort of hairpin bend, following a clear path steeply downhill. You emerge into a field and should go forward to a metalled drive, but before you do, you must detour left to visit the church of Coombes, your final church stop on this walk.

The setting could hardly be more rural, and one might wonder how the church came to be there at all; there is a suggestion that it might have been a hermit's cell. The church has a Norman interior divided by a simple chancel arch – the chancel is thought to date from about 1200, while the chancel arch and the nave are early Norman – and the east window dates from the sixteenth century. It was mercifully left alone by the Victorians. Its chief treasure is its twelfth-century wall paintings of the Lewes Cluniac School, only uncovered in 1949. With many shades of red and yellow with black and white, the paintings depict both humans and animals, including the Lion of St Mark above the arch and, inside the arch, a monstrous man with an extraordinarily exaggerated mouth, crying out as he endeavours, Atlas-like, to support the masonry with which he is burdened. Simon Jenkins puts it beautifully: 'He crouches like a caryatid under the chancel arch, his mouth open in agony and his body fiercely contorted under the weight of the architecture, wonderfully alive to his onerous predicament.' If you packed too much in your rucksack before you set out, you'll know the feeling …

Now it only remains for you to get back to Steyning. Return to the field and go forward to the metalled drive, turning right. Follow it to the T-junction and you will reach the road linking Botolphs with the A27. Turn left and follow the road almost due north for just a few hundred yards, going uphill. At the top of the rise, turn left onto a signed footpath. You go downhill to begin with, then climb, proceeding north-westwards on a field-edge path and enjoying nice views of the South Downs to the east of the Adur including the masts on Truleigh Hill. Keep to the left-hand edge of the field. Follow the signed path through a gate, bearing left to climb briefly to reach a T-junction with a wider track. Turn right onto the track – you are now on the South Downs Way for a brief period – and follow it to a T-junction with a road. Turn left onto the road. You are left with a walk of about a mile back into Steyning, passing through the little village of Annington.

To begin with there is a fairly rural feel to this road walk, but as you climb and pass the junction with Maudlin Lane that leads off to your right, the road takes on a distinctly suburban feel and you long to be back in Steyning. In due course you reach a T-junction – an old signpost proclaims the road you are about to reach to be the A283, whereas the A283 now bypasses the town – and you turn left at the T-junction to proceed into the town centre. This really begins once you have passed Dog Lane that leads off to your left, and very soon you will see Church Street going away to your right. Truffles is a bit further on along the main street on the right-hand side. So, the choice is between celebratory tea and cakes, or a quick dash to the library to find out what a caryatid is.

Chapter Eleven

Best Hilltop Walk

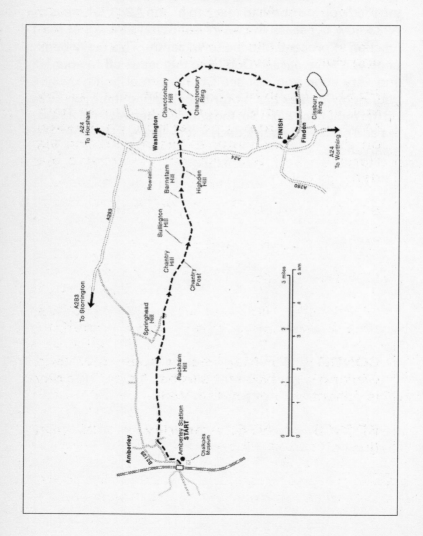

ACCESS BY CAR: Amberley is reachable from the A24 at Washington by the A283 to Storrington and then the B2139, or from the A29 at Whiteways Lodge, just beyond Bury and Bury Hill, by the B2139.

PUBLIC TRANSPORT: There is a railway station at Amberley with two trains an hour Monday–Saturday (one per hour on Sunday) on the London Victoria–Portsmouth line via Horsham and Billingshurst. Bus routes are detailed below.

START: Amberley Railway Station.

FINISH: Findon village centre.

LENGTH: 9 miles.

DURATION: Allow 4 hours, longer if you take time out to explore Amberley and Findon.

CONDITIONS: Magnificent open downland walking with two stiff climbs. A clear fine day is essential to enjoy this walk.

REFRESHMENTS: Amberley, Washington (just off route), Findon.

Sussex is richly blessed with ridgetop walks, most of them on the South Downs Way. The walks from Truleigh Hill to Devil's Dyke, Ditchling Beacon to Blackcap and Itford Hill to Alfriston all offer excellent hilltop walking. But for sustained excellence in terms of views, with two viewpoints that are generally acknowledged as among the best in southern England, and villages at either end which rank among the prettiest in the county, the walk from Amberley to Findon via Chanctonbury Ring and Cissbury Ring is the most rewarding of them all.

This is a linear walk, and therefore you will need to rely on a second car to pick you up at the end, or public transport. Trains from Portsmouth, Chichester, Ford and Arundel (to the west) and Horsham and Crawley (to the north) call at Amberley every hour, and there is a good bus service between Findon and Worthing which connects you back up with the rail network. Note, however, that if you decide to leave your car at Amberley and rely on public transport back again, you will need to catch a bus from Findon to Worthing, take a train to Ford and change at Ford on to an Amberley train. Or you can catch a bus from Worthing to Arundel and change there on to an Amberley train. If you are very lucky you may find a bus travelling direct from Worthing to Amberley but these tend to be summer only. If you are very unlucky you may find that the Worthing to Ford line is closed for engineering works, with replacement buses. Might be just as easy to walk back the way you came ...

Your hilltop walk is mostly, but not all, on the South Downs Way. This is one of the earliest of the long-distance footpaths known as National Trails, passing through areas of outstanding natural beauty or historical interest. The South Downs Way begins at Eastbourne and finishes at Winchester; at least, according to the official guidebook it does, but personally I have always thought it works better the other way, with the Seven Sisters and Beachy Head as its wonderful climax. Though it is now primarily a recreational route, the tracks forming the South Downs Way were once important routes for settlers and traders, and for farmers, who still use the tracks today to transport cattle and sheep.

Between 500,000 and 12,000 years ago small numbers of people occasionally wandered the South Downs to hunt, but the first 'official' settlers were the Neolithic people roughly 5,000 years ago; these were a tribal people who kept animals and cleared trees to grow crops, changing the Downs from forested hills to a more open landscape. Later, the high tracks on top of the Downs became an integral part of the Bronze Age trading network which included the transport of jet, gold and amber. Farming was also important to the economy of the Bronze Age and the ensuing Iron Age, and even now there is still some evidence of Bronze Age farming in the downland landscape. During the Iron Age the population grew, and the downland Iron Age settlers built a number of camps and hillforts, around 300–200 BC, which can still be seen today. It is suggested that these forts, consisting of circular banks and ditches, arose out of tribal rivalry, and in Chanctonbury Ring and Cissbury Ring you will see two outstanding examples of such forts.

Subsequently the Downs were colonised in turn by the Romans, the Saxons and the Normans, and hamlets and villages were established. Farming remained the principal industry of the Downs, and so it remains to this day. However, the leisure industry has assumed a greater importance as walkers have come to love the open downland and its glorious unspoilt surroundings. With well-defined tracks the whole way along, the Downs are popular not only with walkers but also with horses and cyclists. The tracks are not always pushchair friendly, although my ten-month-old daughter seemed quite unfazed by the bouncing of the wheels off the exposed flints and the tilting of the pushchair to negotiate the deep ruts!

You begin at Amberley Station. Before beginning, you may well wish to visit the fascinating Chalkpits Museum across the car park from the station, and detour to either the riverside and its tea gardens (turning left out of the station yard) or to the charming village of Amberley itself (turning right out of the station yard and continuing for about half a mile to a left turn). The Chalkpits Museum is built on the site of an old chalkpit and limeworks and concentrates on the area's industry; there is a good collection of narrow gauge engines, several workshops and a fine array of electrical items. The tea gardens nearby provide a delightful place for you to enjoy a cuppa before setting off, and there is a good pub on the other side of the road.

The village of Amberley is dominated by its castle ruin. The castle, dating back to the twelfth century, was not so much a defensive fortification as a summer residence for the medieval bishops of Chichester, but during the late fourteenth century, when there was a very real threat from the French, Bishop Rede enlarged the palace, building a great curtain wall to protect the north side of the Arun Valley. Even today the high south face of the castle maintains a superb setting close to the river Arun. Much of the church of St Michael dates from shortly after the Norman Conquest and is the work of Bishop Luffa, who built Chichester Cathedral. The church is renowned for its wall paintings dating from the twelfth century, and among the monuments is a brass of a knight wearing the armour of the Agincourt period.

The houses in the village are a happy mixture of timber, brick, stone, thatch, tile and, of course, flint. The Black Horse pub, where you may wish to refresh yourself before setting off, has a collection of hand-carved crooks, sheep bells and a letter from Lord Selwyn-Lloyd, Speaker of the House of Commons in the 1970s, telling of his completion of the South Downs Way. While in name-dropping mode, Charles II is said to have spent a night in Amberley Castle in October 1651 following his exile after the Battle of Worcester.

The hilltop walk begins by your turning right out of the station yard onto the B2139 road and following the roadside, bending sharp left and ignoring a track going straight ahead on the bend. Very shortly you reach a right-hand turning, High Titten. Take this turning and proceed steadily uphill along the road. You are now on the South Downs Way. As you gain height, you can look down to the right at the Chalkpit Museum exhibits. In half a mile you reach a T-junction with Mill Lane. Turn right onto the lane, and very soon reach a South Downs Way sign pointing you off the road on a path to the left. You will now keep to the South Downs Way all the way to Chanctonbury Ring and beyond.

There follows a not overlong but very steep climb up on to the top of the escarpment. Ignore tracks leading off to the right and just keep plugging away. The consolation is that the views are getting better and better all the time, but keep a sharp look out ahead as this is a favoured spot for mountain bikers who race down this hill at a tremendous speed. Finally, the path levels out as you get on to Rackham Hill with the large earthwork known as Rackham Banks, and a little further on is the triangulation point of Rackham Hill – and what a splendid reward you get for your efforts.

A quite tremendous scenic pageant opens out before you. To the left, you can look out across the Arun Valley, the broad river meandering along the valley floor, to the east of which is a huge expanse of fine Sussex countryside with its fields and large patches of woodland, while to the west the South

Downs re-assert themselves, the elegant green slopes rising high above the valley pastures. To the right, you get a tremendous snapshot of the coastline round Bognor Regis and Littlehampton, and a magnificent view of Arundel Castle. You are now 163 metres (535 feet) above sea level, compared with just 4 metres (13 feet) where you began.

Once you are on the top of the escarpment it is very easy walking indeed, and you can enjoy magnificent views on both sides. I particularly love the views to the seaward side, and identifying the coastal settlements as each is passed. To the north you get an excellent view of Parham House, a fine Elizabethan mansion full of splendid paintings and needlework, in the beautiful grounds of Parham Park. You continue on to Springhead Hill, then drop slightly and walk beside a car park, which lies at the end of one of only two roads which meet the South Downs Way between the end of High Titten and the A24 crossing. Not surprisingly, this particular stretch is very popular with those anxious to get the best views for the minimum amount of effort, but it does provide those of limited mobility with an excellent taste of the delights of the South Downs Way. A left fork here – not on your route – leads to the triangulation point at Kithurst Hill.

You then climb again, shortly reaching the other 'road end' at Chantry Post on Sullington Hill. Chantry Post is exactly that – a finger signpost that in recent years has suffered damage but it is to be hoped that when you visit the post will once again bear all its fingers. There are tremendous views here, both north and south. A detour down the road will take you to Storrington, although it is an unexciting little town, and unless you need the amenities a town can provide, it is perhaps better to wait until Washington for refreshment.

BEST HILLTOP WALK

You continue on along the southern slopes of Sullington Hill, getting good views to the tiny village of Sullington and its very small Saxon church. Not half a mile beyond Chantry Post is a fork of paths. Be sure to take the left fork here, leading you on to Barnsfarm Hill, where a left turn provides an alternative route into Washington for horses, avoiding the A24 road crossing.

If you wish to visit Washington, it makes sense to follow this route, which heads north-eastwards across fields and proceeds steeply downhill to arrive at a track at the hamlet of Rowdell. Turn right onto the track and proceed eastwards over the A24 into Washington.

If you wish to omit Washington, keeping to the higher ground, simply continue along the main South Downs Way route from Barnsfarm Hill, dropping down to the A24 via Highden Hill from which it is possible to see the square tower of Washington Church to the east, and the large seaside resort of Worthing to the south. The very busy A24 is a rude shock after the tranquillity and the majesty of the South Downs and you may have to wait some time before you can cross safely. Having got over, you'll probably feel as though you need a pint in Washington anyway!

Washington, despite its American-sounding name, does in fact get its name from the Saxon for 'family of the settlement of Wassa'. It is a pleasant place with a good variety of buildings. Building materials include the traditional downland flint and dark brown sandstone from the Weald, a rolling lowland landscape of fields and woodland that separate the South Downs from the North Downs. The building that I suspect will interest you most will be the Frankland Arms, where walkers are welcome and portions are generous. The beer here found particular favour with the well-known Sussex writer Hilaire Belloc.

The church, with its splendid tower, does have some early thirteenth- and fourteenth-century work, but its restoration in 1867 was described by Pevsner as 'hard and unlovable'. The architect responsible, Gordon Hills, is no friend of Pevsner; other churches in Sussex he restored have been described by Pevsner as 'terribly restored', 'terribly treated', 'appalling restoration', and 'totally and grossly altered'. He must have had his bad points as well …

The 'main' route, following the A24 crossing, turns very briefly north onto a road which, if followed, swoops down to Washington, but rather than descending, fork almost immediately right onto another road signposted 'South Downs Way' and shortly you reach a car park and information board. (If you have detoured to visit Washington, you follow the main street south-westwards from the pub, keep climbing south-westwards and then swing just east of south, now almost parallel with the A24, but at the top of the hill, rather than swinging westwards to hit the A24, turn hard left – almost back on yourself – and shortly you reach the car park and information board.) A South Downs Way sign points you eastwards through the car park, and you follow the South Downs Way on from there. You follow what is an obvious track uphill, passing through an area of woodland, then rise to a T-junction of paths at which you turn left. Proceed now on a clear path to the hilltop assembly of trees known as Chanctonbury Ring, just a few hundred yards ahead.

This Iron Age hillfort, consisting of a ditch and rampart in the shade of a grove of beech trees, is one of the best viewpoints in the whole of southern England, with vast areas of the Weald visible to the north, and, on a good day, views as far as Selsey Bill to the south. Immediately to the north is Wiston House, an Elizabethan mansion set in a lovely park. The trees on Chanctonbury Ring were planted in about 1760 by Charles Goring who lived in Wiston House, but many were blown down in the Great Storm of 1987. Curiously enough, those on the outer fringe fared best, and the storm did bring one bonus: the discovery of a prehistoric human leg bone, found under an uprooted tree. Despite the storm damage it is still a wonderful place. I have mixed memories of it: I recall seeing one New Year in here, and marvelling at the fireworks throwing blazes of colour into the skies above the coastal towns, but also remember hobbling, almost incapacitated, past the Ring one September afternoon having already walked twenty-two miles that day in a brand new pair of shoes. Ouch!

From Chanctonbury Ring you proceed south-eastwards and, keeping thick woodland to your left, drop down steeply to a junction of paths just under half a mile from the Ring. You leave the South Downs Way, by turning right. Ignore a path going off almost immediately hard right and proceed initially uphill, then begin to lose height gradually, heading just west of south. This is delightful open walking.

In half a mile you reach a small area of woodland where a path comes in from the right. Continue on in roughly the same direction, the trees offering some welcome shelter on the very hottest days, and you soon come to a major junction of paths. Go straight over, keeping in virtually the same direction, onto a deeply rutted track. You can see Cissbury Ring straight ahead of you now, and the views to the surrounding downland are quite magnificent.

In a few hundred yards you reach a public car park. You turn right onto the road here to proceed downhill to Findon, but before doing so you will want to visit Cissbury Ring. Cross straight over the road and through a gate where footpath signposts point straight ahead and to the left. Take the path going straight ahead, then continue across a track and up to a kissing gate. Pass through the gate then continue along a clear track and up some stone steps. At the top of the steps, simply keep walking straight ahead to the summit and forward to the triangulation point, with more magnificent views.

Cissbury Ring is another Iron Age hill fort, the largest on the South Downs, surrounded by a ditch and rampart over a mile in circumference. It is believed that over 50,000 tons of boulders, chalk and soil would have had to be moved to construct the fort. The remains of Neolithic flint mines have been discovered here, dating back some 6,000 years.

Having returned to the road by the same route, you now descend to Findon along the road, involving a walk of about a mile. Following a steady descent, you arrive at a T-junction at the foot of the hill, and turn right into Nepcote Lane. In less than half a mile you reach a crossroads which is effectively the centre of the village. There's a bus stop just to your right, where frequent buses leave for Worthing. Just over the road is what is arguably Findon's most impressive building, namely the Gun Inn. The original building dates from the mid-fifteenth century and by 1619 it had become known as the Muskett Gunn Inn.

The village church, which contains a rare thirteenth-century oak screen and medieval oak pews, stands beside Findon Place, an eighteenth-century house in wooded parkland, but both are only accessible by crossing over the busy A24. The village is a very popular base for horseriders, with riding stables to be found close by the tracks leading onto the Downs. Besides the Gun, there are other eateries in Findon where you can celebrate the completion of your hilltop walk; one particular Italian restaurant in the village delighted us a few years back by offering a little-known dessert named 'Mudge Pie'. Bon appetit.

Chapter Twelve

Best Waterside Walk

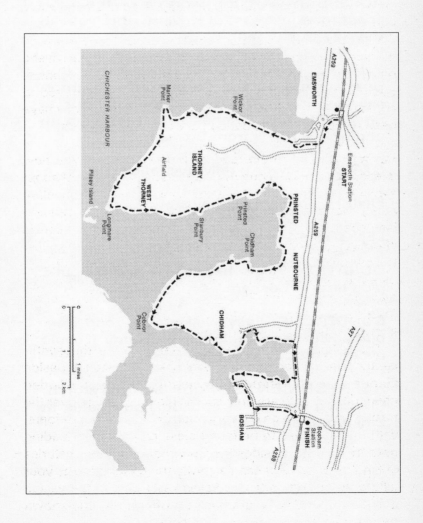

ACCESS BY CAR: Emsworth is on the A259 coast road just east of Havant, and close to the A27 trunk road.

PUBLIC TRANSPORT: Emsworth and Bosham are on the Portsmouth–Brighton railway line, with two trains an hour to Emsworth from Chichester and Portsmouth and hourly trains from Bosham.

START: Emsworth railway station.

FINISH: Bosham railway station.

LENGTH: 14 miles.

DURATION: Allow between 4 and 5 hours, plus time in Bosham.

CONDITIONS: Easy walking on good clear paths with no route-finding problems. It could become muddy in wet weather.

REFRESHMENTS: Pubs at Emsworth, Chidham (off route) and Bosham: cafés at Emsworth and Bosham.

BEST WATERSIDE WALK

Surely, the conventional wisdom has it, the best waterside walk in Sussex should be alongside one of the great Sussex rivers, such as the Arun or the Cuckmere. Certainly a stroll beside these waterways is pleasant, peaceful, picturesque and rewarding. However, such walks do not boast the great variety of scenery, wildlife and history that can be enjoyed by a walk round Chichester Harbour. The walking is very easy, the footpaths always clear and well defined, and you have as your ultimate objective one of the prettiest villages in Sussex.

The walk begins at Emsworth Station, which is actually in Hampshire, albeit only a few hundred yards inside it. Leave the station and turn right onto North Street, right in the heart of Emsworth itself. This pleasant town, with its many attractive old buildings, used to be a very significant fishing port, although it was also well known for its milling and shipbuilding. Continue down North Street to the junction with the A259 where there is a roundabout. Don't go under the subway, but bear left and proceed along the A259 eastwards, crossing the border back into West Sussex. To the right is the millpond that served one of Emsworth's four mills; this particular mill, known as Slipper Mill, was constructed in 1760.

Soon you come to the Mill Pond public house on your left, and at this point you cross the A259. Do so carefully, as this is a very busy road, then almost immediately turn right off the A259 down Slipper Road. The road dies away fairly quickly but you keep going in the same direction over an area of gravel. This takes you to a very large marina with a considerable range of pleasure boats. You keep on in the same direction, passing to the right of the harbour offices – part of which, when I walked this route recently, was occupied by a wood carver – then soon arrive at a junction of paths, signed both left and right. Your way is right, and you follow the path between an assortment of boats; you soon arrive on a track that you follow to the right, and very shortly you come to the waters of Chichester Harbour. Now turn left onto the waterside path.

Chichester Harbour, which you will have for company for the whole of the rest of your walk, was formed following the last Ice Age by rivers of snowmelt and thawing permafrost. The stone and gravel conveyed by the rivers resulted in the harbour bed being scoured out; as the sea level rose, the strip of water we now know as the English Channel came into being, and the harbour was born. You can enjoy fine views across the harbour to Hayling Island and the causeway linking the island with the mainland, and try to visualise the time when these waters were full of vessels bearing flour and malt.

To begin with you can choose whether to take a ridge-top path, which is evidently the better option, or a rather broader but lower one which runs parallel with it to the left. Both paths, however, terminate abruptly at a somewhat forbidding fence and locked gate, part of the inevitable protective paraphernalia associated with the Thorney Island military base. In order to have the gate unlocked for you, you need to press a red button and confirm your identity through an intercom system. It may also be an opportune time for you to come clean about the nuclear missile you have secreted among your tuna and cucumber sandwiches.

Having successfully negotiated the fence and gate, you now continue along the waterside path, on what was once an actual island, and is still known as Thorney Island today. Thorney Island was cut off from the mainland by a modest strip of water rejoicing in the somewhat formidable name of the Great Deep, and over the years the landowners, who made a fairly modest living from the soil of the island, saw the sea make even further inroads into it. In 1870 a decision was made to reclaim nearly two hundred acres of land from the sea. As part of the reclamation, a strip of land was created which had the effect of linking Thorney Island to the mainland to make it effectively a peninsula. The land reclamation turned out to be a massive milestone in the history of Thorney; by the end of the nineteenth century the population had risen by over fifty per cent from what it had been in 1861.

Far more significant, however, was the decision of the Government, in response to the threat of Nazi aggression, to create a new military air base on the peninsula, reachable by an access road which had been made possible by the land reclamation. The RAF moved in during 1937. One of the first civilian establishments to suffer was the school, which had to close in 1938 because it was in the path of the new runway. In common with many other air bases, the base on Thorney Island was attacked on a number of occasions during 1940, until the Luftwaffe began concentrating its operations on civilian targets, and in response to the attacks it was deemed necessary to install false landing lights on the Nutbourne marshes to the east. After the war the RAF stayed on and did not leave until 1976, being replaced by the Army, and the base served in the interim as a lodging for a group of Vietnamese boat people. It remains an Army base to this day, with a medical centre, a school used principally by the children of servicemen, leisure facilities, and shops.

As a civilian walker, you are put firmly in your place by the line of yellow posts that marks the route; it is important to keep to the path on the water's edge, not just because of the fear of incurring the wrath of the military if you were to go outside them, but on account of the most unappetising and uncompromising terrain you would find there.

Notwithstanding the hazards to the left, this is a most

pleasant and straightforward walk; Chichester Harbour to your right makes a very attractive scene, with Hayling Island remaining clearly visible across the water. In due course you arrive at Marker Point, which sounds very important and significant – not many corners on the coastline of West Sussex have the honour of being named – but this merely marks a swing in a more easterly direction, which will certainly be welcome if you have been buffeted thus far by south-westerly winds.

You then swing south-eastwards, and for the one and only occasion on this walk, there is the feel of a coastal walk, with waves encroaching on to the shores at high tide. You are in fact still some way from the open sea here. Keep to the path and don't be too worried when it temporarily parts company from the water's edge, going round the landward side of an area of fairly thick vegetation. This can be muddy, as I found to my discomfiture when I did this walk on a miserable January morning after a period of sustained rainfall. Shortly, however, the path does return to the waterside and continues south-eastwards to the southernmost and easternmost tip of Thorney Island, known as Longmere Point.

Longmere Point is one of the loveliest spots on this walk and indeed on the Sussex coastline, with really excellent views in all directions. Naturally your eyes will firstly be drawn out to sea, and the great sweep of the Manhood Peninsula ahead of you; there are many splendid coastal features along it, and it culminates in the famous sand spit known as East Head which is clearly visible from Longmere Point. However, equally impressive, if not more so, are the views to the beautiful wooded hills that make up the Kingley Vale Nature Reserve to the north-west of Chichester.

Just in front of you is Pilsey Island, which is well known, in common with the whole of Chichester Harbour, for its very considerable variety of bird life. Visitors of the feathered variety include oystercatchers, ringed plovers, dunlins, curlews, shelducks, sandwich terns, red-breasted mergansers, wild swans and brent geese. Meanwhile, there is a good variety of plants as well, which include sea lavender, glasswort, sea purslane, horned poppy and sea holly. One of the most rewarding sights, particularly on a wild winter's day, is seeing a flock of wild geese as they congregate on one of the vast areas of flat fields close to the waterside, and then take off together in close formation. Somehow a grey leaden sky and a bitter wind add extra potency to the sight. Yet it is well documented that Pilsey Island has attracted fowlers who thought nothing of finishing off up to a hundred geese or more in a single bout of gunfire.

Proceeding from Longmere Point, now heading northwards but sticking to the waterside path, you go past the runway of the old airfield, one of the most important reminders of Thorney's comparatively recent history. As you go northwards, keeping to a path that at times may be muddy, you may see an Army tank being driven along the runway, and looking ahead, you will see the buildings belonging to the Army base. You now approach the island's Sailing Club, effectively the chief leisure facility on Thorney, and at high water it will be necessary for you to pass to the landward side of the club buildings, past the church of St Nicholas.

This church is Thorney's most interesting building. Founded in 1100 by Bishop Warlewaste, only a small section of the original church can still be seen today, and most of the structure you see before you is late twelfth and thirteenth century. However, Norman windows still remain, as does a raised cylindrical Norman font. The church is notable for its unusual length (120 feet by 20 feet), and the massive tower at its western end, which was once, it is believed, a store for smuggled goods. The churchyard contains the graves of soldiers and airmen of several nationalities who lost their lives during the Second World War. It ceased to be used as a parish church in 1981, and is now a chapel of ease used by the Army. One curiosity about the church is that it was known as the church of the parish of West Thorney, whereas in fact it lies on the east side of the peninsula.

You now have an easy walk along a clear waterside path that takes you back out of the restricted area, with a red button that you must press to unlock the gate and ensure your release. You go over the Great Deep, which, as stated earlier, is not as formidable as it sounds, and on to Thornham Point, once effectively on the tip of the much less extensive peninsula. You proceed past Prinsted Point and through the Thornham Marina, a popular base for leisure craft, then continue to Prinsted, the village street coming down to meet the coast path. There are seats available for you to sit and admire the delightful views, which include the spires of Bosham Church and Chichester Cathedral.

Prinsted, meaning 'place of pears', is a beautiful village with some of the most attractive cottages on the Sussex coast. There is evidence of life in the area stretching back over 2,000 years, and it is reported that Roman coins and pottery have been found here. Many of the houses have features thought to date from the sixteenth century, and the names of the houses themselves – among them The Thatch and Little Orchard Cottage – are picturesque in themselves and suggest an idyllic and unspoilt community. The oldest and prettiest part of the village is round the meeting of a Y of lanes, in the middle of which are two thatched cottages forming a tiny square, while up the left branch of the Y are two timber-framed cottages with overhanging upper storeys.

The village has a proud association with traditional industries such as agriculture, market gardening and fishing; at one time there was an excellent supply of cockles and winkles in Prinsted Bay, although fishing has now effectively ceased hereabouts and sailing has become the most popular marine pursuit in the area. This is a convenient place to break your walk if you feel that you have had enough; you are now over halfway to Bosham, and Southbourne with its railway station is easily reachable by continuing up Prinsted Lane (the right arm of the Y) to the A259 road. To get to the station, turn right onto the A259 then left into Stein Road. Though you will probably feel as though you have done a great deal of walking already, the sad fact remains that from here to Emsworth via the main road is no more than a mile.

You now proceed agreeably on round an inlet between the Thorney peninsula, which you have just left, and the Chidham peninsula immediately ahead of you. This is excellent walking on a firm path atop an embankment supported by very solid-looking boulders. About half a mile from Prinsted, and shortly before you get going on the Chidham peninsula, there is an opportunity to visit Nutbourne. In the Middle Ages there was a busy port here, and some centuries later it was recognised as a busy and important agricultural community. It is recorded that there was a mill at Nutbourne as far back as 1086, and that a tide mill was built here towards the end of the seventeenth century, standing on an embankment at the north-eastern ear of the inlet named Thorney Channel. Even today, if you look closely, you can make out the remains of the hard where barges used to come up to load and unload at the mill. The mid-nineteenth-century miller was a versatile chap in that he also did business as a coal merchant.

Towards the end of the nineteenth century attempts were made, as at Thorney, to reclaim some of the drowned land; the mill pond was drained, and the mill closed. The reclamation did not succeed, but some good has emerged in that the soggy marshlands are now designated as a local bird sanctuary and nature reserve.

Now you embark on the Chidham peninsula, the second of the two peninsulas the rounding of which makes up the bulk of your waterside walk. Continue along what is an obvious coast path and proceed down the peninsula towards Cobnor Point, enjoying good views back across to Thorney Island. Although the path is initially excellent, it soon deteriorates markedly (although it may have been improved by the time you walk it) and you may be forced down to the beach, where irregular slabs of concrete provide a kind of surface, although even these are not always easy to walk on.

The shores off the west side of the Chidham peninsula contain some of the most primitive signs of human habitation that have been discovered round the harbour, with recent excavations suggesting that man has been here since approximately 2000 BC. Along the western shore of the Chidham peninsula flint scrapers were discovered, suggesting spear shafts or fish traps were made here. Research also demonstrates that Iron Age settlers here created a kind of crude saltern, using very small lined pits to trap sea water.

Your coast path rounds Chidham Point – look to your left for good views of the Regency Cobnor House – then swings south-eastwards towards Cobnor Point; the path peters out for a while, and you will have to walk on the shingle. Fortunately your battle with the shingle is short-lived, as you soon come to a flight of steps which take you up on to a path constructed by the Chichester Harbour Conservancy and designed to be wheelchair friendly.

You pass round Cobnor Point, and it is from here that you will obtain super views across Chichester Harbour to Itchenor, one of the primary sailing centres in Chichester

Harbour and indeed on the Sussex coast. You feel as though there really ought to be a ferry to whisk you across the waters for lunch in the village pub! In fact the only ferry link across Chichester Harbour from Itchenor is with Bosham, and that service has not always been reliable, the boatman having been forced to row the boat on the not infrequent occasions when the motor broke down.

You must now briefly leave the waterside to pass through a grassy area on the landward side of some houses, but a signed footpath soon leads you back to the water's edge. There now follows easy and most pleasant walking, with fine views across the water to Bosham. At a small inlet you reach the metalled Harbour Way, turning left here and following it to a T-junction where you turn right to follow another road.

If you turn left at this T-junction you will reach Chidham. This is a pleasant but not especially attractive community, although there are some interesting buildings which include the restored Tudor Chidmere House, a manor house that dates back to the eighteenth century, a well-preserved farmhouse that is dated 1759, and the attractive thirteenth-century Church of St Mary. There is a link here with Steyning, described fully in the Best Church Walk chapter, in that the church contains a chapel dedicated to St Cuthman; it is suggested that his celebrated journey to Steyning, pushing his mother in a wheelbarrow, began at Chidham, and Cullimer's Field on Cobnor Farm nearby was described as St Cuthman's Field in 1635. There is also a link with one of Chichester's most historic buildings, Edes House, for John Edes, a maltster who was responsible for commencing this building, is buried in the village. Your thirst may be quenched at the Old House at Home, a deservedly popular pub.

Early in the nineteenth century, efforts were made to

reclaim some drowned land between Chidham and Bosham to the east, and in 1812 an embankment wall was built between the two shores. The efforts were doomed, for in 1822 a heavy storm flooded the reclaimed area and it was once again lost to the sea; it is hard to believe that any future efforts would succeed.

As stated above, you turn right at the T-junction to continue, joining the road initially, but you are quickly able to join a path that runs along a parallel embankment on the right-hand side of the road. While the road continues northwards, the embankment path bears right to proceed alongside the shore, with the buildings of Bosham making a delightful sight across the creek which is known as Bosham Channel. The failure of the Chidham–Bosham embankment path means your having to swing northwards, all the way back to the A259. At the time of writing the embankment is impossible to follow right the way back to the main road from here, but immediately to the left you can join a very obvious parallel path which returns you to the extremely busy A259 route. On reaching it, turn right and walk beside it. You have now completed your walk round the Thorney and the Chidham peninsulas and walked nearly 13 miles since leaving Emsworth, so perhaps you shouldn't look at the signpost telling you how far Emsworth is by road, as it might depress you.

You continue alongside the A259 to the north-east tip of Bosham Channel, and immediately beyond it keep a close eye out for a flight of steps and a footpath sign on your right. You go down the steps and take this signed path which almost at once goes back to the shore and follows beside it, heading resolutely for Bosham on what is the last leg of your journey. The way is easy enough to follow, but can get rather muddy, particularly along the field edge.

Progress now depends on the state of the tide: if the tides are favourable, you can walk right along the shoreside to reach Bosham Quay and then join Shore Road which brings you round to the end of Bosham Lane, giving access to the village's shops and other amenities. At high tide, it may be necessary for you to turn left into Westbrook Field, right into Brook Avenue and right again into Bosham Lane, bringing you to the junction with Shore Road.

Ironically, it is possible that when you arrive at Bosham, the culmination of your waterside walk, you will find that you are not actually beside any water at all. The creek beside which it stands, set well back from the sea and effectively an inlet of Chichester Harbour, is tidal. Normally the water covers the creek twice a day at high tide, but at low tide the waters disappear altogether. However, when the waters do rise, the effect can be remarkable, especially when heavy rainfall coincides with high spring tides. Those most likely to be taken by surprise by the changing tides are visiting motorists, many of whom have innocently left their cars on Shore Road and returned to find them almost completely submerged.

Bosham is one of the prettiest villages in Sussex and indeed Southern England, and the church of the Holy Trinity is one of the most important and oldest sites of Christian worship in the county. The earliest part of the present structure dates back to before the Norman Conquest with a significant amount of early-eleventh-century work. It boasts a Saxon tower and chancel arch, and there is a superb Early English east window of 1120 and crypt that was built around the same time. King Harold took communion at the church shortly before the Battle of Hastings.

According to legend, Canute, who became king of England

in 1016, lived for a time in Bosham and had a daughter who was buried in the church. After Canute's death, Bosham became the principal seat of the family of Godwin, earl of Wessex, and the lands were inherited by Harold in 1053. Although the original manor house disappeared a long time ago, there is still a manor house in the village, mostly seventeenth-century, which is almost certainly on or very close to the site of the original Saxon and medieval manor houses.

Despite there being few surviving ancient buildings in the village, there are some seventeenth- and eighteenth-century houses, and as you potter around the quay you will admire Quay Mill, operational until the 1930s and now used as the headquarters of the Bosham Sailing Club. Bosham used to be an important fishing port, with many fishermen amongst those who lived in the village. At the beginning of the twentieth century, only Whitstable outranked its importance to the oyster trade, although it has always been rather overshadowed by Emsworth as a port.

Bosham was at one time an important centre for shipbuilding, and sailing is now the principal maritime activity hereabouts. Incidentally, the old fishermen's cottages bore such august names as Bosham Castle and Bosham Abbey, and it is reported that one young man travelling by train from London confided in a fellow passenger that he was staying in Bosham Castle and was worried in case he did not have appropriately smart clothes to wear!

To get to the railway station, it is necessary to follow Bosham Lane away from the waterfront, passing Bosham Walk craft centre and its excellent tearoom, then continuing past an old Nonconformist chapel and the Millstream Hotel. Beyond the Millstream, pass Critchfield Road and then turn left into Delling Lane, following this to a roundabout where you meet your old friend the A259 yet again. Go straight over the roundabout and just up the road from there you reach the railway station and the end of the walk. There is a good range of amenities round here, in what is known as New Bosham. If you feel like a slap-up celebratory meal, there is an excellent Indian restaurant, and the Bosham Farm Shop will oblige you if all you want is an ice lolly and a packet of Hula Hoops.

Chapter Thirteen

Best Family Walk

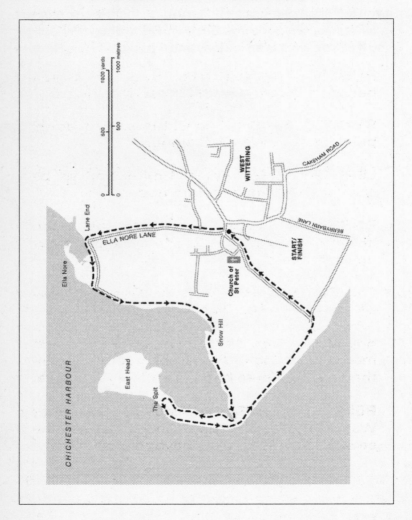

ACCESS BY CAR: West Wittering is reachable from the A27 at Chichester via the A286 and the B2179 (please note that this route is incredibly popular on summer weekends).

PUBLIC TRANSPORT: Regular buses between Chichester and West Wittering.

START & FINISH: The Old House At Home public house, West Wittering.

LENGTH: Approximately 3 miles but can be shortened and/or split into two.

DURATION: Can be walked in little more than an hour, but with children or pushchairs, allow up to 3 hours.

CONDITIONS: Easy level walking, but may be a little wet underfoot in places. It is suitable for pushchairs unless the weather is hopelessly wet. NOTE: This walk is much more rewarding in the winter months, when there will be more bird life and fewer people.

REFRESHMENTS: Old House At Home at West Wittering, Harbour Chalet café on the second half of the walk beyond East Head.

This walk has something for all the family. Adults will enjoy the splendid scenery of Ella Nore and East Head and interesting architecture in the form of St Peter's Church, West Wittering. Children will enjoy the proximity of the sea and the sands, and watching the crashing of the waves and the activity of the surfers. All the family will appreciate the wildlife, particularly the vast numbers of birds that congregate on the shores. And yes, there are plenty of refreshments, from full Sunday lunches to ice creams and tooth-rotting beverages.

Your walk begins at the Old House At Home pub, right in the centre of West Wittering. This has an excellent reputation for its atmosphere and the quality of its food, and crucially it is also family-friendly. Fortified by a meal or a snack in the pub, cross over the main road and follow Pound Road briefly. Very shortly on the left you will see a toilet block, with a seaward road going off to the left. Don't take this road, but take the road going off to the right, directly opposite, called Ellanore Lane. At first this is a rather nondescript narrow metalled road, passing modern housing, but once you have left the houses behind, the surface becomes rougher and the surroundings become more rural. On a clear day you should see a line of hills on the horizon to your left; they belong to the Isle of Wight.

Continue on, and as you do so you will see the waters of Chichester Harbour directly ahead of you. Just before you reach the water's edge, you will notice a path going off to the left, with a gate wide enough for pushchairs. Proceed through the gate to follow the path that runs parallel with the water's edge; at first you are shielded from the water by vegetation, but you can get good glimpses of the harbour and Ella Nore (about which more below) through the breaks. Be warned that this path can get very muddy in wet weather, the first excuse for the younger members of the party to have a whinge.

Soon you reach a small open space with a seat to your left and an information board to your right. From here you can get a good view of, and access to, Ella Nore. This is a shingle spit which juts out quite a long way into the harbour, getting thinner as it goes, and between the spit and the shore there is an area of saltmarsh which boasts a very considerable variety of plants and birds. Plants include sea lavender, cord grass, sea campion, yellow-horned poppy, glasswort, sea purslane, sea beet and golden samphire. Birdwatchers will keep a look out for the curlew, redshank, dunlin, shelduck, mallard, goldeneye, red-breasted merganser, oystercatcher, egret and tern. It is fair to say that the winter sees the greatest variety of bird life. From the open space there are really lovely views across the harbour, which may be dotted with boats at any time of the year.

You now have a choice of paths to get you to Snow Hill, the next (and rather larger) open space on the walk. They run virtually parallel with one another from the Ella Nore information board. The left-hand one is perhaps more pushchair friendly, but the right-hand one is that much closer to the shore, offering fine views to the spit of East Head which is your next major objective on this walk. You can also see further west to Hayling Island, the peninsulas of Thorney Island and Chidham are visible to the north-west, and you have the pleasing prospect of Kingley Vale Nature Reserve beyond.

Very soon you will reach Snow Hill, an open area of green, the name of which is something of a misnomer. There are certainly no hills about here, and lying snow in this area is extremely rare! This area was once a port and a base for fishing, with ten fishing vessels based here in 1817, and it is possible that the Romans had a coastal defence here. The green provides an ideal spot for a picnic, for games or simply to relax and enjoy the surroundings.

The route of your walk continues over the green by the waterside, swinging in a more south-westerly direction, but by following the left-hand edge of the green to its far corner you will be able to pick up Coastguard Lane. This provides easy access back to West Wittering for anyone who has already had enough, or who requires further sustenance at the Old House At Home before making further progress.

Having followed the green by the water's edge you continue to a small inlet and then along a really excellent waterside path, with a further attraction on the left for youngsters to enjoy in the form of a crab pool. The path then has to veer slightly away from the water, again separated from it by an area of vegetation, and indeed as it continues to the next 'staging post' of the walk, namely the neck of the great spit of East Head, it might be easier for those with pushchairs to use the field to the left of the path which may be slightly kinder to the wheels.

On arrival at the neck of East Head, there is another choice to be made: you could simply go straight ahead, up on to the bank, and turn left to follow the shore, omitting East Head altogether. But the recommended route proceeds on to the spit, following a really excellent sandy path along its south-eastern edge. East Head is a huge spit of sand, which, like Ella Nore, has been formed and shaped by the surrounding seas. As recently as the eighteenth century the spit pointed south-westwards out into the Solent, and the entrance into Chichester Harbour from the Solent was just 300 yards wide, but now the spit points north-eastwards, slightly away from the sea. In 1966 the spit was taken over by the National Trust, who planted marram grass among the dunes to prevent the sea washing them away, and it remains an important area for certain birds and plants. Feathered visitors in winter include the dunlin, sanderling, grey plover, godwit, brent goose and teal, but at any time of year you might see a black-headed gull, redshank, cormorant, heron, mallard and oystercatcher. Amongst the dunes you will find a number of plants that thrive in a sandy environment, including sea holly with its thick waxy skin, marram grass which can grow through a metre of sand a year, sea spurge, and sea sandwort. On a clear day, the views from the spit are tremendous; you will see as far afield as the Trundle, well to the north of Chichester, and you can also identify Butser Hill on the South Downs near Petersfield, although it is fair to say the best views are from the far end of the spit, where pushchair manoeuvrability is not easy.

Following the good path as described above, you soon reach a boardwalk going off to the left, which you need to take, but I really recommend that you follow the sandy path as far as it goes; you will note as you continue that the sand becomes softer and therefore more difficult for pushchairs to negotiate. However, it is worth going as far as you are able, especially if the seabirds provide one of their spectacular free shows. In close formation, they will congregate on the sands and then take off as one in a single graceful movement, soon changing direction in spectacular unison before diving back to the sands once more. It is a fascinating sight for all the family to enjoy, and a real miracle of nature.

Assuming you have detoured along to the end of the firm sandy path, return to where the boardwalk leads off, and use it to climb into the area of dunes which make up the 'centre' of East Head and which, with no restrictions on access, provide a paradise for energetic children who will love playing amongst the soft sands.

Shortly, another boardwalk goes off to the left, and you need to take this left turn. Soon, you take another left turn and follow the boardwalk back to the neck of the spit of East Head. This is a lovely little stretch of path, giving you a grandstand view of the waters of Chichester Harbour on both sides of the spit. It is, however, the scene to your right that will interest you more, as this is the point where the comparatively calm waters of Chichester Harbour are met by the open sea. On a stormy day – if you are brave enough to venture out – this is a great place to watch the huge waves crashing against the shore. Further entertainment is provided by the surfers who regularly congregate here and engage in their own cat-and-mouse games with the often ferocious incoming tides.

Having reached the neck of East Head once more, you now simply proceed along an obvious path along the back of the beach, keeping the open sea to your right. This is delightful walking, with views, on a clear day, to the Isle of Wight. If you have not lost the children among the dunes, you may just do so as they rush down to the firm sands or into the sea itself; this area is hugely popular with bathers and beach-lovers and will be absolutely packed at summer weekends, so if you choose a Sunday in August to come here, don't expect to be on your own. That is, assuming you found a place to park your car to begin with.

As you walk, keep a look-out for the Harbour Chalet restaurant to your left. This is a large, unmissable building which, when I walked this route, was easily identifiable by a flagpole and Union Jack. A detour off the bank to the restaurant will be rewarded with welcome cups of tea, ice cream and more solid refreshment if you decided to forgo a meal in the Old House At Home earlier.

Return to the bank and pass to the seaward side of a line of beach huts, then, having left those behind, look out for a slipway to your left, beside the buildings of the surfing club. Make your way up the slipway into a car park, then walk through the car park to arrive at the access road linking West Wittering with the car park for East Head. Turn right onto the access road and follow it back to West Wittering. You somewhat smugly pass the pay gate – assuming you parked on the main street in the village for nothing, or came by bus – and then continue, heading more decisively away from the sea, using a footpath that runs parallel with the road. Look out, on your right, for the distinctive Cakeham Tower, a sixteenth-century construction of red brick and a useful navigation point for seamen.

In due course you reach a T-junction at which you turn right and follow the road. Do spare a few moments, however, to visit the church of St Peter which is to be found on the left-hand side of this road. Believed to have been built by St Richard of Chichester, it has a particularly fine exterior and the interior is certainly worth exploring. The north nave wall is eleventh century, and there is a thirteenth-century chancel, south chapel and coffin lid. The church has one other curiosity, namely the tomb of a so-called boy bishop. Boy bishops were choristers who, in the Middle Ages, were chosen as mock bishops for three weeks or so before Christmas, each fully robed and treated as though they were real bishops.

Return to the road and follow it to its junction with Pound Road. Straight ahead at the junction is Ellanore Lane, but your way now is right, back to the Old House At Home just a few yards ahead of you over the main road. There may be time for a quick stroll in the pleasant centre of West Wittering before you leave. On the opposite side of the road from the Old House At Home is Elmstead, where Henry Royce of Rolls Royce fame had his home. He lived here between 1917 and 1933 and actually discussed and planned the Rolls Royce engine here. But for those who aren't as fortunate as he is, and do not have this lovely area for their home, it's now a long, slow crawl back to civilisation …

Chapter Fourteen

Best Nature Lover's Walk

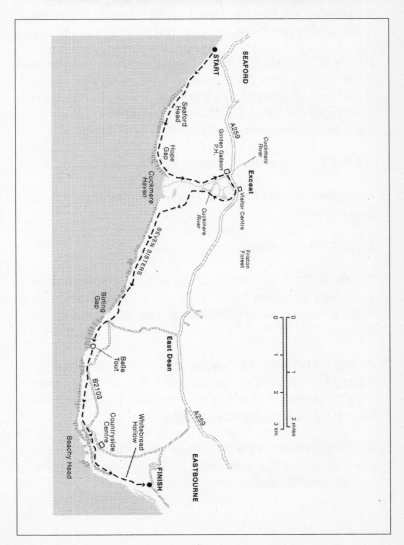

ACCESS BY CAR: Seaford is on the A259 Brighton to Eastbourne coast road, 4 miles east of Newhaven.

PUBLIC TRANSPORT: Regular train services operate between Brighton, Lewes and Seaford. Regular buses run between Eastbourne and Seaford, and train services operate between Eastbourne and Lewes.

START: Sea end of Dane Road, Seaford.

FINISH: South Downs Way start/finish point, Eastbourne.

LENGTH: 9 miles.

DURATION: Allow 6–7 hours; although the walking should take you no more than 4–5 hours, there are many features of interest en route.

CONDITIONS: This is a tough walk, mostly along cliffs, with a good deal of climbing, but it is both exhilarating and rewarding. A clear fine day is a huge advantage.

REFRESHMENTS: Exceat (Golden Galleon pub and visitor centre), Birling Gap, Beachy Head and Eastbourne.

BEST NATURE LOVER'S WALK

The eastern end of the South Downs and the countryside immediately surrounding it is a paradise for those with an interest in the natural world. There is a huge variety of flora and fauna to be enjoyed in this very unspoilt part of Sussex, and even if you can't tell rosebay willowherb from mauve knapweed, or a skylark from a jackdaw, you will still be able to marvel at the extraordinary way in which nature has fashioned this landscape, and to study the uneasy and often tempestuous relationship between the cliffs and the sea. If the weather happens to be stormy on the day you walk it, you might just find yourself witness to the next chapter in this fascinating story.

This is a linear rather than circular walk, so if you arrive at Seaford by car, you will have to choose between retracing your steps or using public transport in order to be reunited with your vehicle. My suggestion is that you use Lewes as a base for the walk; there is a good train service between Lewes and Seaford and, at the end of the walk, from Eastbourne back to Lewes. Lewes is a fine old town with a castle ruin, many historic buildings including the sixteenth-century Anne of Cleves' House, an excellent museum, and large numbers of antique shops and antiquarian bookshops. If you wish to make a weekend of it, you might consider spending one day enjoying the walk described below and the other day pottering round the streets of Lewes. I don't recommend you attempt both in a single day!

Seaford is a pleasant but undistinguished seaside town, the Norman church of St Leonard being the only building you may wish to make a particular point of exploring and, having visited the church and checked your supplies (there are no shops at all en route), you will probably be anxious to be on your way. Having followed Dane Road from the centre of the town to the seafront, you turn left to follow the Seaford promenade. The front contains few hotels or shops, and the buildings you see are predominantly residential; the only feature of real interest is the martello tower, one of many such towers that were erected along the Sussex coast for defensive purposes. This one is now a local history museum.

You get to the end of the promenade at a car park, which is at the foot of the cliffs, and then embark on quite a tough cliff climb that takes you to Seaford Head and its nature reserve. You can choose between paths that keep a clear course between the cliff edge on the right and the golf course on the left. Already you can see the continuing influence of nature on these cliffs; they have been subjected to erosion in the recent past, and it is important that you stay well back from the edge.

The reward for your efforts is your arrival at Seaford Head, the site of an Iron Age hillfort, from which there are fantastic views of Brighton to the west and the enchanting prospect of the Seven Sisters and the Cuckmere Valley ahead of you. A good track on springy turf now provides a clear walk across the cliffs. You are now walking across part of Seaford Head Nature Reserve, the 308 acres of which comprise not only downland but also mudflats and meadowland; it is home to over 250 species of plants and a large amount of wildfowl.

Still enjoying wonderful views ahead of you to the Seven Sisters, you now start to lose height, keeping to this very good path, and eventually arriving at Hope Gap. Even if your knowledge of natural history is very limited, you will not fail to be impressed by the beauty of the surroundings or the wonders of nature in creating this superbly secluded spot in a valley between rising cliffs. Unless the weather is unkind to you or you are in a great hurry, I thoroughly recommend that you detour down a flight of steps to the rocky pavements separating the cliffs from the sea, for it is here that you get your best opportunity on the walk to view at first hand some of the marine flora and fauna that lie off the Sussex coast.

To return to your walk, you turn left at the foot of the slope, ascending to a rather less spectacular cliff top. Staying on the cliff path, you proceed towards a small grouping of houses, which erosion has brought rather too close to the cliff edge for comfort. Passing to the left of them you reach a clear track at a right-angle to the cliff path you have been following, then bear right onto the track and descend, going to the left of the houses, eventually reaching a gate. You are now at Cuckmere Haven, a small plain sandwiched between cliffs at the mouth of the Cuckmere River.

Ignoring the arrow pointing left, go straight through the gate and carry on to the shingle beach, heading towards the cliffs on the other side of the beach. The way forward is soon obstructed by a channel of water, and it is here that you turn left to join a clear path that takes you along its west bank, heading inland. Although in a way it is disappointing to leave the cliffs behind, there is ample compensation in the form of lovely views across Cuckmere Haven. Just be warned that it could be muddy after rain!

Although it is perhaps less easy to see from your valley-bottom path, the final passage of the Cuckmere river to the sea is noteworthy for its spectacular meanders. The mouth of the river has moved east because of encroachments of the shingle beach, and a new cut was created in 1846, strengthened by automatic weir control, to avert the danger of flooding. Although it is believed that King Alfred founded a shipyard at Cuckmere Haven, the mouth of the Cuckmere is today one of the most unspoilt river mouths in the south-east of England, and is the only river valley in Sussex to provide wildfowl with a natural merging of meadow marsh, saltings and a wild seashore.

There is an artificial lagoon behind the raised shingle bank of the beach which attracts ducks and waders such as the coot, mallard, moorhen, shelduck, redshank, dunlin and ringed plover, while the sheltered waters of the meanders may attract cormorants and herons in summer and tufted ducks, dabchicks and Canada geese in winter. Other birds you may see hereabouts include the curlew, peregrine falcon, hen harrier, greenshank, redstart, shoveler, yellow wagtail, garden warbler, whitethroat and common and green sandpiper, black kite, yellowhammer and Dartford warbler.

In due course you reach the Golden Galleon pub, one of four refreshment opportunities on this walk, and continue through the pub car park. This brings you to the busy A259, and you turn right to follow beside it, soon crossing the bridge over the water. Thankfully a roadside footpath is available. Just beyond a sharp right-hand bend you reach Exceat visitor centre, the gateway to Friston Forest. The centre not only provides a restaurant and tearoom but also has attracted visitors for many years with its excellent exhibition on local wildlife and a very impressive series of live insect displays. It also provides an ideal base for exploration of the forest, if you feel you have time for a detour. Its 1,500 acres contain over 4 million trees, and it is one of the largest beech woodlands in the country. Delights of the forest include two orchids, the white helleborine, which flowers in May, and broad-leaved helleborine, at its most impressive in August; the yellow bird's nest plant, which blooms in July; the pheasant's eye, a rare plant whose crimson red petals and dark purple centre are at their best between May and August; and a large number of butterflies which include the small tortoiseshell, speckled wood, meadow brown, white admiral and wonderfully-named grizzled skipper!

BEST NATURE LOVER'S WALK

Assuming you have explored the visitor centre and Friston Forest, cross back over the road. More or less opposite the visitor centre there is a metalled track leading seawards away from the A259, and it is this track you now take. It is protected by a gate which bears the sign 'Residents And Authorised Vehicles Only', but pedestrians can gain access to the track through a smaller gate to the left. Simply follow the track back towards the sea; it is from this track that you get a rather better view of the amazing meanders of the Cuckmere estuary to your right. At weekends and holiday periods throughout the year do not be surprised to be one of many walkers enjoying this excellent path, which is suitable for pushchair and wheelchair use.

In about half a mile the path swings quite sharply left, away from the valley and up towards a cluster of farm buildings. Do not go left with it, but fork right here onto another path, which is signposted 'Seven Sisters Cliffs/The Beach'. You make your way through a gate, and then after about 100 yards you fork left. Initially this left fork path remains on the flat, but then passes through a gate and up a flight of steps. You continue forward to a fence and may be tempted to go over the stile in the fence that you soon reach, but don't do so; simply carry on walking parallel with the fence, keeping it to your right, and press on uphill on a clearly marked path. This is quite tough going but the views back across Cuckmere Haven are wonderful, and as you gain height you are able to get a better and better appreciation of the remarkable geography of the Haven and its surrounds. For a little while you seem to lose the fence, but continue in the same direction on a clear path, crossing a stile, and soon you're reunited with the fence again.

At length you reach a fingerpost at which you turn left, along the path signposted 'Birling Gap' and now find yourself on the crest of the first of the Seven Sisters cliffs. Take one last opportunity to enjoy the amazing views to the Cuckmere Valley and the downland beyond. There now follows some quite magnificent walking as you tackle the Seven Sisters in turn, sharp descents followed by stiff climbs, but taking care to keep well back from the cliff edge.

The Seven Sisters, seven spectacular chalk cliffs, form the eastern end of the South Downs and the climax of the South Downs Way, the course of which you are now following and will continue to follow for the rest of your walk. They owe their origin to geological activity between 50 and 100 million years ago. Each clifftop or 'sister' has a name: in turn they are Haven Brow, Short Brow, Rough Brow, Brass Point, Flagstaff Point, Bailey's Hill and Went Hill Brow. The depressions separating each 'sister' are what is left of the valleys of ancient rivers.

The walk is a treat for all nature lovers. Patrick Coulcher, in *Unto The Hills*, writes of the Seven Sisters: 'How often have I sat here amongst the downland flowers and watched early summer sea mists creep up and dance above these scalloped cliffs and seemingly with their soft embrace touch the very heart of nature itself.' Sadly, because of the grazing activities of the local sheep, plant life on the Seven Sisters is not as abundant as it once was, but if you look carefully you may see viper's bugloss, cowslip and field fleawort in profusion where grazing has ceased, while the unspoilt chalk hills continue to attract a number of birds including the jackdaw and the fulmar petrel. The fulmar has been visiting the cliffs between Brighton and Hastings for a number of years, and is identifiable by its very distinctive poise in flight, its long narrow wings, frequent periods of gliding, and guttural croak. However, arguably the loveliest creatures to frequent the high cliffs are the butterflies, including the red admiral with its distinctive red bands and white markings, the clouded yellow with its shades of orange-yellow and black, the marbled white, and five species of blue.

Coming down from the final Sister, you make your way through a gate and carry on along a clear wide track, soon reaching a T-junction of paths, then turn right to proceed along another wide stony track downhill. At the bottom you hit the road and simultaneously arrive at Birling Gap, a freak cleft in the South Downs, with its big car park, pub and café immediately to your right. You have to enter the car park briefly to proceed, but in fact you exit from it almost at once by passing to the left of the telephone kiosk. If conditions are favourable, it is possible to detour to the beach and walk beneath the steep chalk cliffs, and indeed it is said that the best way of truly appreciating the grandeur of these cliffs is to see them from the shore.

The shore immediately below the cliffs is draped with fronds of seaweeds like bladderwrack and serrated wrack, while in the rockpools you will see not only red and green seaweeds but brown serrated wracks, beadlet and dahlia anemones, shore crabs, hermit crabs, possibly squat lobsters, limpets, razorshells, egg-cases of whelks and dogfish, and, at low tide, seaslugs, prawns and breadcrumb sponges! While this is a fascinating place, it is also potentially dangerous, for if the tide engulfs the beach you have no means of escape. Take immense care not to get cut off.

Having passed the kiosk you begin climbing again, and you have a choice of paths to take you up to and along the clifftops, aiming for the Belle Tout lighthouse. Do note that the South Downs Way is signposted to the left of the lighthouse, and I suggest you take this route yourself. The Belle Tout lighthouse was built around 1830, but proved rather ineffective in the thick mists that crept in from the

English Channel and hung between the clifftop and the sea. It was subsequently replaced by a sea-level lighthouse just off Beachy Head and became a dwelling, but owing to cliff erosion the building has had to be moved more than once, and may have to be moved again.

Plants to be found in the vicinity include the field fleawort, early purple orchid, early spider orchid, all of which are at their best in April or May, and small hare's ear, which flowers in June or July and is extremely rare, this being one of only two locations in Britain where it can be found (the other being Berry Head in Devon). During the nineteenth century, people ground up dried tubers of the early purple orchid and mixed it with hot milk, honey and spices to create salep, thought to have aphrodisiac properties!

There follows a steep descent to meet the road at a small car park, and beyond that you embark upon the long but exhilarating climb towards Beachy Head. The grass is really good to walk on and the views get more splendid with every step, with the high-rise buildings of Brighton easily discernible on a clear day. At length you reach the summit, 535 feet above the sea, and with a terrifyingly long and steep drop to the waters below. If you do decide to make for the cliff edge to view the lighthouse and the sea, take enormous care.

The name 'Beachy Head' has nothing to do with any beach but is derived from the French 'beau chef' meaning 'beautiful headland' (rather than 'good-looking cook'). On the clifftop is the Beachy Head Countryside Centre, which concentrates on downland life and includes several wildlife displays. The wildlife and plant life on Beachy Head is quite magnificent. Since 1990 it has once more become a breeding ground for falcons, and it is one of the best places in Sussex to see the stone curlew. Other birds you may see here include the dark-grey-winged herring gull, jackdaw, rook, rock pipit, fulmar, guillemot, tern, crag martin, chaffinch, bullfinch, fieldfare, collar dove, great black-backed gull, lesser black-backed gull, crow, lapwing, linnet, pied wagtail, owl, starling, swift, whinchat and greater-spotted woodpecker. On the ground you may see a fox, badger, common lizard, slow worm, grass snake, adder, hedgehog, mole, foxcub, grey squirrel, vole, shrew and, of course, the ubiquitous sheep.

Plants that may be found on the edge of the cliffs include bellflower, mauve knapweed, scabious, pink centaury and betony, while about 20 of the 50 or so species of British butterfly have been seen here, including not only our friends the red admirals but cabbage whites, brimstone, meadow/wall browns, chalkhill, painted lady, skipper, green hairstreak, dark green fritillary, and blues including the famous adonis blue. Ironically it is nature itself that poses the biggest threat to these magnificent cliffs; as recently as January 1999 there was a major cliff fall, or, as Patrick Coulcher put it, 'another piece of England broken away to be dissolved into a nothingness'.

When you arrive at the observation point a little before the summit, stay on the ridge and aim for the triangulation point, but before you get to it, and just before you get level with the hilltop Beachy Head Restaurant, turn right onto a metal path. Shortly the metal path describes a big loop, with a seat at its bottom end. Take the short cut across the loop using the path provided, but having done so, instead of turning left onto the metalled path again, pass straight over it onto a path that contours the hillside. Do not continue forward on this path, but turn right immediately, just before the footpath signpost that includes the South Downs Way acorn symbol, to join a broad green track which descends very steeply. From this track you can enjoy fantastic views ahead to Eastbourne and the coastline beyond, and in clear conditions you will see the buildings of Hastings in the distance.

Keep on the wide track all the way to the cliff edge. When you reach it, turn left to follow the green clifftop path; it is lovely walking, with the sea to your right and Whitbread Hollow to your left. A number of interesting plants are to be found hereabouts including purple rosebay willowherb; bird's-foot trefoil, the flowers of which provide a magnificent carpet of yellow in early summer; the tall viper's bugloss with bell-shaped blue and purplish-red flowers; the early gentian with its blooms of pale purple; the red valerian with its red and white flowers and subtle fragrance that makes it popular with butterflies and other insects; and the sea radish, which produces four-petalled yellow flowers that appear in summer. Look out also for cowslips, orchids, harebells, bellflowers, pheasant's eye and possibly more: it is estimated that unless it becomes overgrown, this downland turf contains 46 species per square metre!

Having enjoyed a splendid cliff-edge promenade, you rise to meet a wide gravelled track, on to which you turn right. The track soon becomes a metalled road, with housing now separating you from the sea. You descend to a café marking the end of the South Downs Way, and the beginning of Eastbourne.

The most pleasant way to the centre of Eastbourne is to turn right beyond the café into Duke's Drive and follow it downhill. You pass Helen Gardens, then just beyond these gardens you bear right along a road signposted Holywell, Promenade (Western Parade). Keep along this road, ignoring turnings off to the right, and you will shortly arrive on the promenade. Turn left and simply follow the promenade into Eastbourne, passing the martello tower known as the Wish Tower, and a

BEST NATURE LOVER'S WALK

Lifeboat Museum. Devonshire Place, just past the massive Cavendish Hotel, offers the most convenient access to the town centre.

Even in this bustling town the glories of nature can be readily enjoyed, not only in the banks of flowers which adorn many of the streets, but also in the many delightful gardens, including the well-known Carpet Gardens which have been established in the town for more than a century, and the Butterfly Centre. Here you can walk amongst jacaranda, hibiscus and bougainvillaea and watch as exotic butterflies and moths flutter about freely.

There are many other attractions in the town including the Towner Art Gallery and Local History Museum, the superb architecture of Grand Parade, the Coastal Defence Museum in the Wish Tower, the redbrick fortress known as the Redoubt which also houses a museum, and the How We Lived Then Museum Of Shops. Perhaps the nicest way to end your walk is at the nineteenth-century town pier, from the end of which you can gaze up at Beachy Head and reflect that despite the attraction of this very fine resort, with its buildings and its history, the most impressive sight of all is that presented to you by nature itself. Then, suitably inspired, you can make your way back to the station, endeavouring to remember the difference between viper's trefoil and early purple bugloss.

Chapter Fifteen

Best Coastal Walk

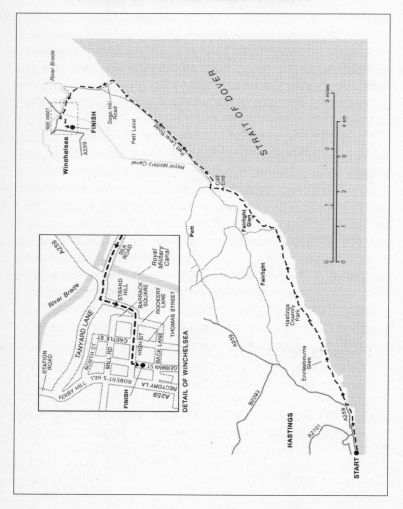

ACCESS BY CAR: Hastings is reachable from London and Tonbridge via the A21, and from Eastbourne (to the west) and Folkestone (to the east) by the A259.

PUBLIC TRANSPORT: Hastings is very well served by trains from London Charing Cross/Tonbridge/Tunbridge Wells, and also by trains from Lewes and Eastbourne. Winchelsea is on the line between Ashford International and Hastings, with a less frequent service. There are regular buses back to Hastings from Winchelsea Beach and Winchelsea.

START: The pier on Hastings seafront.

FINISH: St Thomas Church, Winchelsea.

LENGTH: 9 miles.

DURATION: Approximately 4 hours, but allow a day if you wish to explore Hastings and Winchelsea.

CONDITIONS: The first half of this walk, over the cliffs, is quite tough, with some very steep climbs and descents. The second half is much gentler beach-edge walking.

REFRESHMENTS: There are plenty of refreshment opportunities at Hastings; a pub at Cliff End; shops, pub and restaurant at Winchelsea Beach; and shops, pub and tearoom at Winchelsea. There are no amenities whatsoever between Hastings and Cliff End, and as this is a demanding section you are advised to stock up before leaving Hastings.

If you have successfully completed the Best Nature Lover's Walk between Seaford and Eastbourne, you might be forgiven for thinking that in terms of coastal scenery in Sussex, there is nothing that could beat it. However, whilst it is undeniably spectacular, it does not perhaps demonstrate the tremendous variety of the Sussex coastline. On your walk from Hastings to Winchelsea you will begin at a town which is not only one of the foremost seaside resorts in Sussex, but also has a long association with the sea and is steeped in history; you will enjoy some of the most spectacular coastal scenery in Sussex, arguably surpassing in scenic beauty and majesty even the Seven Sisters; you will spend some time following an area of totally unspoilt seashore, with ample opportunity for dipping your toe in the water as well as looking out for the many different seabirds that frequent the surrounding sands and marshes; and you will end with a village that was once an important port but which is now one of the prettiest and most unspoilt villages in the county.

Hastings is a fascinating town and deserving of some exploration. It was one of the original Cinque Ports and regularly contributed ships to the Navy during the Middle Ages. The old town grew up in the valley between two sandstone ridges, namely East Hill and West Hill. Arguably the most impressive historic remnant of Hastings is the Norman castle ruin to be found on West Hill, from which narrow lanes lead to the centre of the old town. The High Street contains many fine old buildings including several half-timbered ones, and there are numerous narrow alleys or twittens leading off the street. One of these, St Clement's Passage, leads to St Clement's Church, one of just two medieval churches remaining out of seven that existed at one time.

Although Hastings' importance as a naval town was to decline, it has continued to flourish as a fishing port. Evidence of this is to be found not only in the Fishermen's Museum in Rock-a-Nore road close to the seafront, but also the tall, black-tarred wooden huts or 'net shops' where fishermen hang their nets out to dry and store their equipment.

Hastings started to develop as a seaside resort in the early part of the nineteenth century, and with the developers came some fine Regency architecture, perhaps most notably in Pelham Crescent and also Wellington Square. Other attractions Hastings has to offer include St Clement's Cave, a system of underground passages on West Hill; the Shipwreck Heritage Centre, which includes a warship that was beached near Hastings in 1690; the Stag Inn in All Saints Street with its smugglers' secret passage and mummified cats; and the Hastings Embroidery, a sort of modern Bayeux Tapestry depicting 81 scenes in British history during the 900 years from the Battle of Hastings.

The pier, where your walk begins, was completed in 1872 but needed to be repaired after the Second World War, being deliberately damaged to avoid it being of use to potential invaders. Legend has it that the Conqueror's Stone at the head of the pier was used by William the Conqueror as a dining table for his first meal in England!

Proceed eastwards from the pier along the front beside the main road (the A259), noting the fine cream-painted White Rock Pavilion, built in the 1920s, over the road from it. Continue to the Breeds Place roundabout, with its attractive fountain, then carry on beside the main road, walking along the seaward pavement, and passing a boating lake. The road negotiates a sharp bend at the point where it meets Rock-a-Nore Road. Don't go down Rock-a-Nore Road but instead take the next right, along East Bourne Street. You then turn left up All Saints Street, which boasts many buildings of interest including Shovells, a timber-framed house where an admiral lived in the seventeenth century. From All Saints Street you turn right into Crown Lane, and here the hard work begins as you rise steeply; this will be the first of many climbs during the first half of the walk!

Where the road swings left, don't swing left with it but go straight on up a steep flight of steps. You soon arrive at a green with a signboard welcoming you to East Hill, the site of an Iron Age hillfort which is believed to date back to 40 BC and thought to have been the centre for the export of local iron and grain, and the import of wine. You are now in Hastings Country Park. Simply follow the right-hand side of the green, close to the cliff-edge fence, and in due course you find yourself on a proper path.

You now embark on a quite magnificent walk. The country park, much of which has been designated as a Site of Special Scientific Interest, is formed of 540 acres of countryside east of Hastings and your walk will pass through some of the loveliest parts of it, with heather-clad hills, tremendous sandstone cliffs that consist of some of the oldest rocks in the south-east of England, and deep wooded glens. It is all quite different from the cliff scenery between Seaford and Eastbourne.

Leaving the green behind, you continue to climb, enjoying magnificent views back to Hastings and ahead to the country park. But instead of remaining on the clifftop, as you will have done in the course of your conquest of the Seven Sisters, you are now faced with a descent, which in fact is the first of four major downhill plunges on this part of the walk. Ignore paths leading off to the left, but keep the cliff-edge fence to your right. Reaching a gate, you fork right to descend into Ecclesbourne Glen, a wooded valley that was a favoured haunt for smugglers a couple of centuries ago.

Nowadays it is a wonderfully peaceful spot, and it is hard to believe that the busy town of Hastings is quite so close. The thick undergrowth hereabouts is ideal nesting territory for warblers and tits.

Having hit the valley bottom you might be forgiven for hoping for a gentle walk along the flat, but almost at once you find yourself climbing again. Initially the surrounding hillsides might make you feel somewhat hemmed in, but the path broadens out as you make progress upwards, the gradient does ease, and you can again enjoy majestic views. Now you begin your descent to Fairlight Glen, taking the right-hand path at a fork on your descent. (The signposting in the country park is excellent, and if in any doubt, simply follow the signposting for Fairlight Glen.) Described as the most beautiful of the glens in the country park, it is carpeted in spring with bluebells and wood anemones, and a stream flows between great boulders under the tangled trees. It is a wonderfully refreshing spot on a hot day.

When you hit the valley bottom, it is important that you take the right-hand turn along the route signposted Lovers Seat, Coastguard and Firehills. You cross a stream and commence another very considerable ascent. Initially your path swings to the left, and for a while you may feel you are going away from the sea, but reassurance soon comes in the form of a right-hand turn, signposted Lovers Seat and Coastguard. The going is tough, but the severity is mitigated somewhat by a flight of steps that takes you to the wonderful Lovers Seat viewpoint, beside which is a sarsen stone. Close to the viewpoint, a path going off to the left offers a detour to the hilltop village of Fairlight, although it is well over a mile away. The churchyard contains quite an impressive array of tombstones, and Gilbert & Sullivan buffs may wish to seek out the memorial stone to Richard D'Oyly Carte.

From Lovers Seat there is another descent, into Warren Glen, and this plunge is quite a difficult one, as the path is not only steep but stony. Be very careful, and watch where you are putting your feet. There are fewer trees in this glen than in the other glens, but if you look up you will see oak, hazel, beech and ash, and in the moister areas of the glen itself you should look out for alium and golden saxifrage.

Now you are faced with yet another long and strenuous climb, but you can be reassured that there is nothing as tough to follow. The views are arguably the best of the whole walk. This area of the country park, where you will notice a preponderance of heathland, has the rather dramatic name of Firehills; it gets its name from the bright fiery colour of the gorse-covered slopes in summer. The area attracts such birds as the stonechat and yellowhammer, and looking down you may be fortunate (or unfortunate!) enough to spot a common lizard or adder.

Once you have reached the top, you should now have a clear view of the hilltop coastguard station, which will have featured on some of the signposts you have passed earlier. As you head for the coastguard station you will see a gate just short of it: go through the gate and immediately fork right to follow the cliff edge path. This is magnificent walking, and significant too in that there are no cliffs higher than this to come further east along the coastline of Sussex, or indeed the south coast of England. The sadder trivia buffs in the party can try and work out when, if you continued walking anticlockwise round the English coastline, you would next meet cliffs that were as high. Without wanting to give too much away, it's a fair way on from here.

At length, after a wonderful clifftop promenade, you reach another gate. You make your way through it and to begin with you find yourself on a narrow path between fences which widens into a broad stony drive, with the sea to the right and houses to the left – the first habitations since you left Hastings, which will seem a long time ago now. You make your way confidently downhill until you reach Shepherds Way coming up from the left. Although there seems to be a way ahead, subsidence has effectively made further direct cliff-edge progress impossible. You must turn left down Shepherds Way, then right into Bramble Way, going forward into Rockmead Road. This swings to the left, arriving at a T-junction with Lower Waites Lane, on to which you turn right. Initially the road is metalled but does become rougher as you make further progress.

You then turn right into Sea Road and head towards the gate. Just before the gate, however, look out for a narrow path going left off the road, with a National Trust signboard saying 'Fairlight'. You may think this somewhat incongruous, as the turning to Fairlight village was some way back! You join the path and proceed along it, soon climbing again, but be assured that it is nothing like as tough as some of the earlier ascents. It is also the last climb you will have to undertake until you reach the outskirts of Winchelsea.

You go to the left of John's Seat, then simply follow straight along the path as it levels and descends; it has to be said that the cliff edge does sometimes look uncomfortably close to your right. Ignore left forks but keep an eye out for the particularly imposing thatched mock Tudor house to your right. When you reach the foot of the hill, you reach a drive on to which you turn left. Almost at once you will arrive at a T-junction with a road; turn right and proceed along this road through the village of Cliff End as far as the Smuggler Inn, your first refreshment opportunity since you left Hastings.

You turn right into the car park of the pub and walk through it, pass the unremarkable St Nicholas Church, and ascend very briefly to join a promenade. You then turn left to follow it. After so much cliff walking, it is quite a shock to be faced with such flat surroundings. The promenade, such as it is, soon comes to an end, but it is replaced by a firm embankment path that you continue to follow towards Winchelsea Beach.

This is a most pleasant walk, with fine prospects both to your right and left. To your left is Pett Level, the westernmost end of Romney Marsh, consisting of a broad flat expanse of reclaimed land that comprises marsh criss-crossed by drainage ditches and canals. Through it passes the so-called Royal Military Canal, which was constructed as a defensive measure in the early nineteenth century at a time when there was a very real fear of French invasion. A road was built behind it, the Royal Military Road, to allow fast transport of troops and equipment. It is doubtful whether any of it would have been much help in an invasion: as William Cobbett wryly remarked, 'Armies who had so often crossed the Rhine and the Danube were to be kept back by a canal […] 30 feet wide at the most.' The area is now a haven for wildlife and plant life.

To your right is the beach, and there is no reason why, if the tide is right, you cannot follow the sands rather than sticking to the embankment path. At low tide it is possible to see the 7,000-year-old roots and stumps of the remains of a forest inhabited by Stone Age people. A vast number of sea birds have been sighted here, including the spotted redshank, shelduck, widgeon, teal, pintail, tufted duck, lapwing, coot, moorhen, mallard, pochard, black-headed gull, herring gull, dunlin and purple sandpiper.

The shores hereabouts have had much else to offer in the past. In *Off The Beaten Track In Sussex*, Arthur Cooke writes: 'Our beach-loafer "on the find" may stumble across flotsam and jetsam of every kind … There is no shore so prolific as that which begins at Cliff End. After a storm the fringe of beach above high-water mark is strewn with many a child's tiny argosy of cork, with a skewer for mast. These, and quaint oddments of wood, toys, perchance, from the wreck of some merchant vessel; bits of drift-wood, light as touch-wood from years of immersion; now and then a small keg or box – unlike Pandora's – empty, or wreathed with seaweed; all these, and the inevitable basket are but a sample of the gifts of the sea.'

Even if as a latter-day beachcomber you are not as fortunate, you can stand and enjoy the vastness of it all: the great expanse of beach, the sea beyond, the broad marshes, and of course the skies above you. And yes, the silence too – unless the nearby beach suddenly fills up with other hunters of seaweed-wreathed kegs.

As you approach the sprawl of Winchelsea Beach, roughly two miles from Cliff End, a much pleasanter prospect, namely the old hilltop town of Winchelsea, presents itself across Pett Level to your left. Your coastal walk is now nearly at an end. Since Cliff End you have been proceeding parallel with a road, known as Pett Level Road, but as the houses of Winchelsea Beach are approached, the road veers away from the embankment path into the village. Stay on the embankment path for just under half a mile.

You pass the somewhat inelegant Rye Bay caravan park which lies to your left, then just past a large white-painted house, Sea Spray, the embankment path widens to become a fairly broad concrete promenade. Join this promenade and after just a few yards you pass a toilet block, immediately beyond which is a flight of steps. Your sea walk ends here, so pause and enjoy one last look at the sea, with Rye Harbour Nature Reserve to your left and the fine cliffs you have tramped earlier to your right. Then, having bidden farewell to the sea, go down the steps to join Dogs Hill Road, which you follow away from the shore, keeping an area of green to your right. For a short period this was, surprisingly enough, a harbour for shipping, having been trumpeted as 'a new harbour for Rye' because the silting of the existing Rye Harbour was threatening trade. The new harbour was opened in July 1787 after very considerable investment of time, money and manpower, but by November of that year the entrance was blocked with shingle and became unusable.

Continue along Dogs Hill Road; as you reach the T-junction at its end, note the pretty brick-built church of St Richard just to the left. Over the road at the T-junction are some useful amenities including a convenience store and a restaurant. Turn right at the T-junction and follow Sea Road. Soon you reach the Ship pub, outside which is a bus stop with regular buses available to Hastings should you wish to forgo the final mile away from the coast into the main village of Winchelsea. If you wish to continue, walk on along the road for about 200 yards, then look out for a phone box on the left-hand side of the road. Immediately beside the phone box is a grassy footpath heading north-westwards away from the road, and you follow this path. It is a most pleasant stroll, with excellent views to Winchelsea which is now almost on top of you, as well as the shoreline and cliffs you have just left behind. You also briefly follow the bank of what is one of numerous watercourses on the levels between Winchelsea Beach and Winchelsea.

Soon you arrive at a road – it is in fact the continuation of Sea Road – and turn left to follow it. Shortly you pass the delightfully old-fashioned Suttons Fish Shop, where you may wish to purchase a souvenir of your coastal march in the form of some freshly caught fish, and a couple more hundred yards bring you across the Royal Military Canal and on to the junction with the main A259. Turn left onto it, and then take the first road leading off it to the left, signposted Winchelsea. This is Strand Hill, which takes you steeply uphill, giving splendid views across the levels to the sea.

You pass through the splendid old Strand Gate, and swing right into the High Street, crossing St Thomas Street and passing to the right of St Thomas Church. By turning left into German Street you will find not only a convenient entrance to the church but also a bus stop with regular buses back to Hastings. If you prefer the train, continue along the High Street to its junction with Roberts Hill, turn right and descend very steeply to a hairpin bend. On the bend is a left turn, Station Road, which takes you to Winchelsea Station where there are trains to Hastings.

It is hard to believe that Winchelsea was once at shore level, right by the sea, and an important port; the old town stood on a shingle spit on the seaward side of where the town is situated today. By the end of the twelfth century it had become one of the Cinque Ports and early in the thirteenth century was providing ten ships for the English fleet. The old town was, however, largely washed away by a great storm in 1287. Even before the storm, work had begun on a new town, to be built on the hilltop; on the orders of Edward I, it was laid out by the Warden of the Cinque Ports and the Lord Mayor of London with a view to its assisting the wine trade with France. Even today it is possible to see the grid street pattern, making it in effect England's first piece of town planning! Although it was hoped that the new town would develop as a port, as the old one had done – to this end, wharves were built on the banks of the river Brede below the town – the further ravages of nature caused the town to be cut off from the sea, and the port had ceased to function by the fifteenth century.

Although the town was developed only to a fraction of

the size hoped for by Edward I, Winchelsea has a large number of splendid buildings. Perhaps the most impressive old building is the Church of St Thomas. Although the tower, aisles and nave were destroyed by French invaders, you can still see canopied and pinnacled tombs that date back to the early fourteenth century, with Sussex marble effigies. In the churchyard there is a tree named Wesley's Tree, so named because it is the descendant of the tree under which John Wesley preached his last open-air sermon in 1790. The other noteworthy example of a building which has its origins in the first days of the new town is the Court Hall, which contains a museum, while some of the old vaults, which are thought to have served as cellars for the barrels of wine imported from Gascony, are at least 700 years old.

In Castle Street you will find a fourteenth-century house called the Armoury, and in the garden of Greyfriars in Friars Road is situated the ruin of a Franciscan church that was built between 1310 and 1320. Moreover, Winchelsea retains its three medieval town gates, namely the early-fourteenth-century Strand Gate, the early-fifteenth-century Pipewell Gate, and the medieval New Gate.

Although the original street layout remains, the streets are now graced with well spaced out houses that are rather more recent in origin, although many still go back two or three centuries. With the A259 bypassing the village, the overwhelming feeling, especially out of the tourist season, is one of peace and tranquillity, and a sense of timelessness. There is a good mixture of white-painted and tile-hung buildings, many decorated with climbing roses and wisteria. Look out for the eighteenth-century New Inn in German Street and the nineteenth-century Well House in Castle Street. You can also observe the Town Well with its lovely old sign which somehow symbolises the quaintness of the village: 'Notice is hereby given that this well is to be closed at 7 o'clock in the evening and opened at 6 o'clock mornings and to be closed all day on the Sabbath.'

Chapter Sixteen

Best Teashop Walk

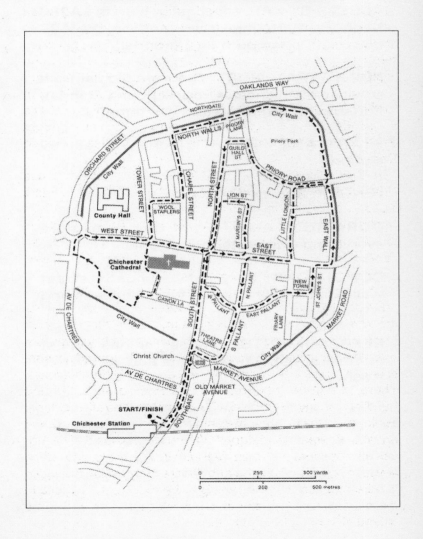

ACCESS BY CAR: Chichester is on the A286 Midhurst–Witterings road, and on the A27 between Portsmouth and Arundel.

PUBLIC TRANSPORT: There are regular train services to Chichester from London (Victoria), Portsmouth, Brighton and Worthing.

START AND FINISH: Chichester railway station.

LENGTH: 3 miles.

DURATION: Allow a full day to explore everything Chichester has to offer.

CONDITIONS: Very easy – mostly street walking. Entirely suitable for pushchairs and wheelchairs.

REFRESHMENTS: Chichester has a vast number of pubs, restaurants and, of course, teashops.

BEST TEASHOP WALK

In many ways this walk beautifully complements the Best Challenge Walk which features elsewhere in this book. If you have successfully completed the challenge, what better way to unwind than by strolling round Chichester for a day, relaxing in one or more of the many delightful teaplaces the city has to offer? Chichester is a wonderful city with so many fine buildings; it is perhaps best known for its cathedral, but there are a number of other historic landmarks and architectural gems to see and enjoy, including the Bishop's Palace, the Cross, the city walls, St Mary's Hospital, the Assembly Rooms, Edes House and Pallant House, not to mention several old churches and a very impressive array of eighteenth-century town houses, all within a surprisingly compact space. The city also boasts one of the finest range of shops in the whole of Sussex.

Chichester is a magnet for pilgrims, artists, historians, tourists and shoppers, so it is perhaps unsurprising that it should have spawned so many splendid eateries and, in particular, teashops. Although this walk will focus in on three, I cannot resist mentioning a number of others along the way, and you may well spot many more that I have not mentioned!

Before you start, a couple of words of advice. Firstly, please note that Sunday is *not* a good day to do any part of this walk, since two of the tearooms featured do not at present open on Sunday, and many of the shops are shut on Sunday as well. Secondly, market forces are notoriously unpredictable and although the teaplaces featured here were all thriving at the time of writing, one cannot rule out the possibility of any (though hopefully not all!) of them ceasing to trade as teaplaces and becoming either posh, upmarket restaurants – as has happened to what used to be my very favourite teashop in Chichester – or, worse still, discount retailers flogging inferior quality toys and bargain packs of underpants.

You begin your walk at the railway station, one of the less aesthetically pleasing buildings in the city. Turn left out of the station forecourt and make your way past the Globe pub and the Job Centre, crossing over the Avenue de Chartres by the pedestrian crossing and continuing in the same direction into South Street. Follow South Street to its end at the Cross, which you will see clearly ahead of you as you proceed up the street. Though far from being the most interesting street in Chichester, South Street boasts a number of eye-catching buildings. On the right as you go up, just past Theatre Lane, is No. 43 South Street, a splendid redbrick building dating from 1792 and formerly a theatre. Next door, No. 44 is a fine flint building that was built about 1820, and just beyond that is the Wren-style Regnum Club that has eighteenth-century features. On the left, as you go up, is the fine archway of Canon Gate, a gatehouse in late Perpendicular style that was largely reconstructed in 1894, and the entrance to the delightful Canon Lane.

A little further up, on the same side, is the flint-built Vicar's Hall, given to Chichester Cathedral for the use of the Vicars in 1394; it stands immediately above a late-twelfth-century vaulted undercroft known appropriately enough as The Crypt. Previously named The Crypt Coffee House, it had at the time of writing become The Buttery, serving a good range of sandwiches, snacks and cakes from a tempting counter display. I particularly recommend the warm cheese scones, which come with generous portions of butter.

You continue on to the Cross, the undisputed centre point of Chichester and one of the most enduring, as well as endearing, features in the city. It was built in 1501 by Bishop Edward Story to enable market traders in the city to sell their goods under cover, and since then it has been used not only for market trading but the making of public proclamations.

If asked to name a particular feature of the Cross, most people will at once think of the clocks, and may not even realise that in a recess on the east face of the Cross is a bust of Charles I. It is in fact a replica of a bust that was made for Charles I in the 1630s, and which itself had previously been placed in the central niche of the Cross.

Turn right at the Cross into East Street. Shortly on the right you will see the Royal Arms, known also as the Old Punch House; it was constructed on the site of a house where Elizabeth I was entertained in 1591, and nearly three centuries later the landlord was appointed manufacturer of Chichester Milk Punch to Queen Victoria. The pub stands on the site of the original St Mary's Hospital, about which more below. Follow East Street then take the first turning on the left, into St Martin's Street. This starts somewhat unpromisingly, with the modern Marks & Spencer on the east side of the street, but a little further up on the left you reach St Martin's Tearooms, the first of three tearooms highlighted in this walk.

As soon as you enter you feel you are stepping into the rather large drawing room of a rural residence two centuries ago, with its subtle lighting, low beams, cosy alcoves, brick and timbered walls, sturdy wooden tables and chairs, and the profusion of flowers. The food is mostly organic and is all home-cooked, free from artificial flavouring, colours or preservatives, and no convenience food is used. Savouries include welsh rarebit, potato cake, mushrooms on toast, open sandwiches with egg or salmon, and a variety of soups including carrot, leek, broccoli, courgette and tomato. There is also a good range of salads. Among the cakes are scones, flapjacks, apricot slices, banana bread, honey and lemon cake and carrot cake, and there is a range of refreshing teas and coffees to accompany your food. There is a wonderful wild garden with tables liberally scattered about it, providing an idyllic spot to relax on a hot summer's day. Be warned, though – it is expensive.

Emerging from the tearoom, turn left and continue up St Martin's Street. Soon you turn left into Lion Street, but it is definitely worth going on a little out of your way to inspect St Martin's Square immediately beyond. It is not so much a square as a widening of St Martin's Street but it is a lovely piece of historic Chichester that has hardly changed over the last century. Highlights include the yellow painted No. 5, known as Candle House, with the impressive redbrick No. 7 opposite; Nos. 20 and 21, which are good eighteenth-century redbrick buildings; and the long low front of St Mary's Hospital, the body of which is best seen later in the walk.

Returning to Lion Street, you now follow it westwards to its junction with North Street, and turn left into North Street. Immediately on the left, as you enter North Street, is one of Chichester's most impressive buildings, the redbrick and pillared Council House, built by the city corporation in 1731 to replace the old Council Chamber. The architect was Roger Morris, one of the principal exponents of the Palladian style, and it is worth standing some way back from the building to appreciate his work.

Continuing on down North Street, you pass St Olave's Church with thirteenth- and fourteenth-century features, since converted into the SPCK bookshop, and further down on the left is Market House, also known as the Buttermarket. Built by Nash in 1807, and added to in 1900, this superseded the Cross as the venue for market trading in Chichester. Proceed on down to the Cross, and this time turn right into West Street.

The cathedral, with its magnificent spire which is visible from many parts of the city and beyond, now comes into full view on your left. Meanwhile, on your right as you follow

West Street, is a row of shops which occupy the site of the former Dolphin & Anchor Hotel, the buildings of which date back to the eighteenth and early nineteenth century. A little further down, past the post office, you reach the Army & Navy, which was once the home of the Oliver Whitby School, built in 1904. If you stand a little back from the store you can see the motto VIS ET SAPIENTIA inscribed towards the top of the building.

There are three good refreshment opportunities along this part of West Street: Hadleys, which is perhaps more of a restaurant than a tearoom, the café in the Army & Navy which offers good value breakfasts and lunches for shoppers, and my own favourite, the coffee shop on the first floor of Waterstone's. It offers lovely views, a bright, cheerful décor, and mouthwatering cakes, including a very acceptable apple and mincemeat shortbread!

Opposite the Army & Navy you will observe the cathedral belltower. The belltower is thought to date from around 1428, and contains a ring of eight bells, the earliest dated 1583. Cross to the south side of West Street and pass the belltower, then turn left, descend some steps and walk across a wide paved area past the west door of the cathedral.

Whole books have been written about the glories of the cathedral, which dates back to the end of the eleventh century, and which is crammed full of treasures including Norman sculptures, magnificent fourteenth-century choirstalls, the imposing fifteenth-century Arundel Screen, the Shrine of St Richard of Chichester, John Piper's altar tapestry and Marc Chagall's stained glass window depicting Psalm 150.

Having passed the west door of the cathedral, continue round an area of green to enter the cloister. Turn right into the cloister then just beyond a noticeboard but before the

Bishop Bell Rooms – which offer very reasonably priced meals and snacks including my favourite, half a roll topped with scrambled egg – turn right down St Richard's Walk, a narrow paved alley; No. 1, immediately on the left, has an eighteenth-century look but in fact disguises a medieval structure and is probably fourteenth century. Follow St Richard's Walk to its junction with Canon Lane, the eighteenth-century Deanery facing you as you reach the junction. Your route is to the right but you may wish to detour left to inspect the thirteenth-century Chantry and another alleyway, the Vicars Close, consisting of fifteenth-century houses.

Having turned right into Canon Lane, continue to its end, go under the archway, and follow an obvious path through Bishops Palace Gardens. The palace itself, situated on your right as you reach the gardens, dates back to the early thirteenth century, and is a magnificent building of brick and flint. Following the path, you reach a T-junction with a wider path and turn left on to this, arriving at the busy Avenue de Chartres. Turn right and almost immediately arrive at a roundabout, at which you turn right into West Street again.

Arguably the two most striking buildings in this part of West Street are the mid-eighteenth-century Marriott House on your right, and the splendid late-seventeenth-century redbrick Edes House to your left. A little further up on the left is the former church of St Peter the Great, built in the mid-nineteenth century. It now houses a bar known as The Toad; formerly, much to the annoyance of many townsfolk, this previously sacred building was called The *Slurping* Toad!

Turn left into Tower Street, following it until you reach the library which is to your left, and here turn right into the Woolstaplers, bearing left at the T-junction to follow Chapel Street; on the left as you follow Chapel Street is Providence

Chapel, built in 1809. You shortly arrive at a T-junction with North Walls. Immediately over the road is a flight of steps leading on to the walls; here you climb the steps and follow the wall eastwards. Pushchair users should simply turn right into the parallel street and follow it to the end.

It is fun to walk along the walls, parts of which date back to AD 100, and to look down at the backs of the neat terraced cottages of Orchard Street, with houses painted green, white and red. You soon arrive at the junction of North Walls with North Street. Cross straight over North Street – the cosy Orchard Tearooms are to be found a little way down North Street on the right-hand side – and proceed along Priory Road. As the road bends sharp right, take a path left to return on to the walls (no problems with pushchairs this time) and enjoy a very agreeable walk along the walls with the green expanse of Priory Park immediately to your right.

In the middle of the park is the former chapel to the Greyfriars monastery, dating from the thirteenth century; the monastery fell victim to the Dissolution and the chapel has subsequently served as a courthouse, a rifle range and a museum. Enjoy also the fine flint walls and colourful painted stonework of the houses of Franklin Place to your left. Proceed along the wall, which offers a good view of the cathedral spire, then at the end drop down to Priory Road. Turn right and then left into Little London with its delightful assembly of eighteenth-century houses, with red brick the dominant motif.

You pass the Chichester & District Museum, and soon afterwards reach Shepherds, now my favourite teaplace in Chichester. There is a lovely bright feel to it, with its light green walls and white china, the staff are unfailingly friendly and welcoming, and the service is extremely efficient. Winner of Top Tea Place of the Year Award in 1990, 1992 and 1995, and presented with a Tea Council Award of Excellence every year since 1989, it offers a dazzling array of teas, ranging from English Breakfast, Earl Grey and Finest Darjeeling to Camomile and Lapsang Souchong. Foodwise, the house specialities are the rarebits: welsh, buck, stilton and tomato, bacon and mushroom, and brie and bacon are all on offer, while sandwiches include brie with cranberry and lettuce, BLT, and egg mayonnaise and cress, and there are jacket potatoes crammed with tuna mayonnaise or garlic mushrooms. To follow, enjoy scones, preserves, cakes and puddings, including their 'roulade of the day'!

Emerging from Shepherds you continue on down Little London to its junction with East Street. Immediately past Shepherds you could detour left into the pleasant covered parade of shops known as Sadlers Walk; in the parade you will find Chives, a cheerful café serving a wide range of cooked meals, sandwiches and cakes. Having reached the bottom end of Little London, turn right into East Street, noting immediately opposite the six-column Greek Doric portico of what is now McDonald's but which was the Corn Exchange, built in 1832. Having turned right into East Street, proceed briefly along this street then turn right up a signed alleyway leading to Chichester Centre of Arts, the former church of St Andrew Oxmarket, built originally in the thirteenth century. From here there is an excellent view northwards to St Mary's Hospital and chapel. The building has served as a hospital since it was vacated by the Franciscans in 1269.

Returning to East Street, follow it westwards then turn left into North Pallant. This contains many fine town houses, Nos. 1 and 16–17 particularly impressive, with arguably the grandest being Pallant House on the left, just before the left turn into East Pallant. Pallant House was built at the start of the eighteenth century for the Chichester merchant Henry Peckham, and it is now an art gallery containing a splendid collection of twentieth-century British art. Turn left into East Pallant, another street of attractive houses of which my favourite is the yellow-painted East Pallant Cottage, then pass the end of Baffins Lane and go straight into New Town, following this road to a T-junction with St John's Street.

Turn left and follow St John's Street, passing St John's Chapel which is to your right. Built in 1812–13, its features include a gallery and a huge three-decker pulpit, and although it is redundant as a place of worship, it is often open to visitors. Follow the street to the end, turning right into East Street and shortly left into East Walls. Until recently, the Shippams factory was situated here, and the old factory buildings line the left-hand side of the street as you begin to follow it. The recommended route is along the wall parallel with this street, from which there is a good view to the attractive houses of East Row to the left, but pushchairs must stick to the road; although you will have no difficulty getting the pushchair on to the walls, you will have a problem at the end!

Descend the steps from the walls and turn left into Priory Road; there are some pretty cottages in this road, which skirts the southern end of Priory Park. Pass the turnings into Little London and St Peters, then bear left into Guildhall Street, noting the impressive Ship Hotel to your right. On your left is our third featured teashop, Clinch's. There used to be a Clinch's in South Street – very sadly, this closed some time ago – but the Guildhall Street Clinch's offers a similar menu and atmosphere albeit under different ownership. The atmosphere is delightful, whether you choose to sit in the same room as that in which the food is served, or whether you adjourn with your food to the conservatory area and sit among the plentiful greenery. The feeling of wellbeing is enhanced by the deep chairs, carpeted floors, pictures, sensitive lighting and classical music. Typical offerings from the open sandwich menu include smoked salmon, prawn, tuna, honey roast ham and cottage cheese. There is a good selection of jacket potatoes including prawn, tuna, cheese and ham; you may instead opt for my favourite at Clinch's, a mini quiche, with an imaginative side salad to accompany it. Puddings are plentiful, with sticky toffee pudding, banoffi, fruit crumble and apple pie to choose from on the day of my visit, or you might opt for a slice of cake, which might perhaps be carrot, chocolate or coffee, or a house speciality, Duke Of Cambridge, consisting of dried fruit and nut with caramel topping: unusual but delicious.

Emerging from Clinch's, you follow Guildhall Street to its end and turn left into North Street, following it all the way down to the Cross. This overlaps a little with ground you've already covered, but you will enjoy the Georgian architecture all the way down. Look out for two gems on the right, namely the flint-built Fernleigh Centre, and the eighteenth-century building occupied by Arthur Purchase with its splendid cantilevered first-floor bay window. No. 37, occupied at the time of writing by Q's hairdressers, also boasts a fine bay window, while to the left as you walk down is the imposing Old Cross Inn.

Having reached the Cross at the bottom of North Street, go straight on over into South Street, retracing your steps for a while, but this time turn left off South Street into West Pallant. This is a delightful little street. On the left is yet another redundant church, All Saints In The Pallant (now occupied by the Red Cross) which dates back to the thirteenth century; No. 5, built in about 1770, which is reminiscent of some of the fine town houses in St Martin's Square; and No. 12 on the opposite side which dates back to the early eighteenth century. At the crossroads turn right into South

Pallant, a pleasant but unspectacular street, then swing round to the right along Old Market Avenue, keeping the modern redbrick Christ Church to your left. Shortly you arrive back in South Street. Cross over and then turn left, retracing your steps. Cross the Avenue de Chartres then simply continue on to the station where your walk began.

Your Teashop Walk is at an end, but with so much to see and enjoy in Chichester at any time you will surely find every reason to return to sample the cheese scones at The Buttery for which you hadn't worked up sufficient appetite, the mushrooms on toast that you spurned in St Martin's, the chocolate roulade you didn't quite have room for in Shepherds, the mini-quiches that Clinch's had just run out of before you got there ...

Chapter Seventeen

Best Challenge Walk

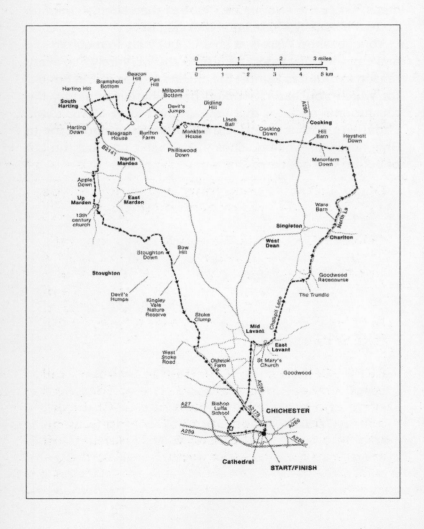

ACCESS BY CAR: Chichester is on the A286 Midhurst–Witterings road, and on the A27 between Portsmouth and Arundel.

PUBLIC TRANSPORT: Regular train services to Chichester from London (Victoria), Portsmouth, Brighton and Worthing.

START AND FINISH: The Cross, Chichester.

LENGTH: 30 miles.

DURATION: A very long day, and can be extended over two or even three days.

CONDITIONS: This is a very long, tough walk. *On no account should you attempt it in a single day unless you are sure you are physically capable of doing so.* The nature of the terrain, and the precautions you should take, are set out more fully in the body of the text of this chapter.

REFRESHMENTS: Chichester is very well served by eateries and food shops. There is a shop and pubs at Lavant, a pub at Charlton, a shop, pub and tearoom at Cocking (just off route), a shop and pub at South Harting (off route), and a pub at Stoughton (off route).

North of Chichester lies some of the loveliest, most unspoilt countryside in the whole of Sussex, with magnificent chalk downland, spectacular hilltop viewpoints offering tremendous vistas of the Weald and the sea, huge acreages of forest, rolling pastures, and secluded villages with fine old churches. It is this countryside that provides the setting for the spectacular circular walk described below, which is far longer than any others in this book. It can be tackled in two ways.

You could decide to spread the walk over two or three days, using Cocking and Harting – both well served by public transport between Monday and Saturday – as places to break off the walk for the night. Alternatively, you could endeavour to complete the whole walk in a single day as a personal challenge; you may even feel you want to use your challenge walk as a basis for fund-raising, with family and friends sponsoring you to complete the task. It's certainly more fun and better for you than other traditional sponsored events such as fasting or sitting in a bath of cold baked beans!

If you do decide to have a go at doing the whole walk in a day, you should be absolutely sure that you are sufficiently fit. A walk of thirty miles, while theoretically achievable in a single day by any fit and experienced walker with sufficient daylight at their disposal, is a mammoth undertaking, especially if – as is the case on this walk – there is a lot of up-and-down work to do. You need at least ten hours to complete the task, so it is best to avoid the winter months. You need a fine day: not only will bad weather make it a much tougher task, but you won't appreciate the beautiful surroundings if it's pouring with rain. You need to wear a good stout pair of comfortable walking shoes or boots, and wear sensible, comfortable clothing. You should start out with adequate supplies of food and drink, not to mention blister pads and plasters, and should not rely on pubs, shops or tearooms being open or available when you want them.

You should also have some sort of back-up available should it become clear that you are not going to complete the walk within the day; it would certainly be prudent, for instance, to carry with you a mobile phone and numbers of local taxi firms. But if you plan carefully, and are properly equipped for the task, you will find this an immensely enjoyable and rewarding walk, even if your nearest and dearest begin to question your sanity!

You begin at the Cross in the centre of Chichester. (The many and varied architectural and historic features of Chichester are described more fully in the Best Teashop Walk chapter.) Your walk begins innocuously enough with a stroll down West Street, keeping Chichester Cathedral and the bell tower to your left. At the end of West Street you cross straight over the roundabout into Westgate, and then follow Westgate away from the city centre, initially passing office buildings and shops, and then impressive residential properties.

You come to a mini-roundabout with Sherborne Road leading off to the right. Go straight over the mini-roundabout and continue along what is a cul-de-sac for vehicles, leading to a pedestrian railway crossing. Just before you reach the crossing, however, turn right at the bus turning area onto a concrete path; a signpost pointing up the path proclaims Lavant to be three and a half miles away. Follow the path to a tall metalled gate, beyond which are the grounds and buildings of Bishop Luffa School. Turn left just by the gate to join the course of the Centurion Way, the southern section of the old railway linking Chichester with Midhurst. The original Chichester–Midhurst railway opened in 1881 and closed in 1953, although the section between Chichester and Lavant remained in use for goods traffic until 1970. This same section was converted into a proper path during the 1990s and now enjoys extensive use by walkers and cyclists. Your challenge walk follows the path all the way to Lavant, a distance of three miles. It is straightforward level walking and good to get some easy miles under your belt before the real work starts! Until the first overbridge, carrying the B2178 Chichester–Funtington road, there is open countryside to the left and, beyond the Bishop Luffa school buildings, suburban housing to your right. Beyond the B2178 overbridge the feel becomes much more rural, with cuttings that are thick with vegetation on both sides and, although there is still housing to the right, there is a feeling of moving out of suburbia.

Two overbridges follow in close succession; just before the second you pass by the picturesque Brandy Hole Copse. Beyond these two overbridges there is modern housing followed by a tall embankment to your right, whilst to your left, beyond a more modest cutting, is a large area of rolling grassland with good views to Kingley Vale Nature Reserve beyond.

Your path then rises to meet the top of the embankment. You pass under the Hunters Race bridge, a signpost indicating a pedestrian and cycle route (not part of the Challenge walk) to Goodwood, West Stoke and East Ashling, and proclaiming that Lavant is half a mile away. Beyond this bridge, the countryside remains open on your left but the houses of Lavant are now to be seen to your right. The path enters a small cutting, goes under a bridge, then very shortly beyond that bridge passes under the A286 bridge. Just beyond the A286 bridge is some modern housing development to your left, including the redevelopment of the old Lavant station building. In its final years of operation the chief product that was loaded here was sugar beet, classified somewhat curiously by BR as 'minerals other than coal'!

BEST CHALLENGE WALK

Your railway walk is now at an end. Immediately beyond the row of modern buildings, turn hard left and double-back on yourself, passing the other side of the old Lavant station building and going up to meet the A286. Turn left, passing over the bridge across the old railway, to follow the road through the sprawling village of Mid Lavant. Very soon, however, take the first left turn along Sheepwash Lane. The road goes downhill and follows alongside the right bank of the River Lavant, which is usually dry in summer but provides an often impressive flow in winter. In 1994 the river burst its banks after prolonged heavy rainfall and caused extensive flooding. To your right is the picturesque village green of East Lavant.

You arrive at a T-junction with Pook Lane, and turn left to cross over the river, continuing past St Mary's Church, which boasts a Norman west door and a seventeenth-century brick tower. Follow the road uphill beyond the church, passing the Royal Oak pub and rows of private houses. Having cleared the houses to your left, you reach a slight right-hand bend in the road and a sign indicating the end of the village speed restriction. On the bend and just before the speed sign you turn left to follow a wide and obvious track, Chalkpit Lane, heralded by the signboard 'Unsuitable for motors'. This is your first piece of really hard work, as you follow a stony track uphill for roughly a mile and a half. You have now left Chichester and Lavant behind and are now out in open countryside.

The views get better all the time; as you climb, you will see to the west the wooded hills of Kingley Vale, which you will be tackling later, while looking back you will get a tremendous panorama incorporating Chichester and its cathedral spire, Chichester Harbour, and the coastline around Bognor Regis and Pagham Harbour. At the top of the hill, you arrive at a car park followed immediately by a crossroads of paths. Turn right here to follow a path which climbs on to the rounded hill; known as the Trundle, it was fortified by local Iron Age inhabitants and is now a very popular beauty spot. With its twin radio masts it is a readily recognisable landmark which can be seen from many miles away, and on a clear day it is possible to identify the Isle of Wight from the summit.

Your route follows the clear path that goes straight over the hilltop, although it is possible and indeed desirable, if you have the time, to detour onto the path that follows the perimeter embankment, from which the best views can be enjoyed. Your direct route, on a good wide track, passes just to the right of the lower of the two radio masts and through a small gap in the embankment, then quite steeply downhill. You have lost the views to Chichester and the sea but the views northwards provide more than ample compensation.

You arrive at a gate, passing through it and turning sharp right, then shortly turn sharp left and descend a flight of stone steps to reach the Goodwood–Singleton road. Goodwood Racecourse is a very short way to the right. Cross straight over the road into a small car park and pass through the car park to join a minor road heading northwards off the Goodwood–Singleton road. Follow this minor road quite steeply downhill, losing all the height you have gained on the walk from Lavant to the Trundle; the road walk is most pleasant, with enticing views to the valley ahead and the wooded hills beyond.

A mile or so from the car park you reach the little village of Charlton, where you meet the river Lavant again. You arrive at a junction with the East Dean-Singleton road; to continue the Challenge Walk, cross straight over into North Lane, but if you turn right along the East Dean–Singleton road you reach the quaintly-named Fox Goes Free pub, an ideal lunch spot, assuming you are planning on stopping for the night at Cocking. If you're attempting to do the whole walk in a single day, you will be in some trouble if you find they're serving lunch when you get here, as you aren't even a quarter of the way back to Chichester!

Having joined North Lane, follow it as it proceeds very gently upwards, the ground either side of the lane rising much more steeply. The lane passes Ware Barn then swings left; ignore signed paths leading off right and then left, but continue along the lane, which then swings right and heads for a large area of forest. Just as the lane is about to enter the forest, it reaches a crossroads of footpaths, and it is here that you must turn left, diving now into the forest along what seems initially to be a rather unpromising path. (Do *not* be tempted along a track that forks immediately left from here along the edge of the forest; it is strictly private and will take you miles off course!) Very soon, however, you will reach a T-junction with a much wider track which is also a public path; turn left and follow the track north-westwards in a dead straight line. Forest walking can be confusing with so many tracks, but on this occasion there is absolutely no need for hesitation as you proceed, simply ignoring all the many crossing tracks, gaining height all the time. On a hot day you will be glad of the shade, as this is quite hard work.

At length you arrive not only on the top of the hill but at the northern edge of the woods, where your path ends at a T-junction with the South Downs Way. Turn left to follow the South Downs Way westwards. You will now follow this national trail, which runs from Eastbourne in East Sussex to Winchester in Hampshire, for eight and a half miles as far as Harting Hill. The waymarking on the South Downs Way is excellent, so route-finding will not be a problem for this stretch!

You join the national trail on Heyshott Down, and, proceeding westwards, you descend via Manorfarm Down. To begin with, you keep the woodland immediately to your left, but you soon leave this behind and continue through more open countryside to the buildings of Hill Barn. From here it is a short, straight descent to the A286 Chichester–Midhurst road; there is a convenient bus stop here with regular buses southwards to Chichester and, over the road, northwards to Midhurst (services run daily, including Sundays). The Challenge Walk goes straight over the road, but by turning right onto the A286 and following it steeply downhill, you reach the village of Cocking, which boasts a shop, pub and tearoom. You may see a sign advertising the pub on the route of the South Downs Way itself, with the tempting offer of 'food, beer and beds'. Who could refuse?

You now face your third big climb of this walk. Having crossed straight over the A286, your route proceeds gently past the north end of a car park which is often very busy, and on past the farm buildings of Cockinghill. Then the hard graft begins, as you climb slowly but surely on to Cocking Down, following a stony chalk track. It is worth turning back to look eastwards towards Manorfarm Down and Heyshott Down, and northwards to Cocking and Midhurst, and the attractive hills beyond. Once you gain the top of the escarpment, you now enjoy a quite magnificent high-level walk, with tremendous views southwards to Chichester Cathedral and the sea, passing close to the triangulation point of Linch Ball and continuing across the top of Didling Hill. The track provides excellent walking, and you really feel on top of the world in every sense, with open pastures immediately around you, heavily wooded slopes falling away beyond them, and a stunning panorama in the distance. Although, ideally, this walk should be undertaken when the days are longer, the best time to be up here is on a crisp sunny day in winter where the view just seems to go on for ever.

Sadly, beyond Didling Hill your trusty track dives into woodland, passing close to Monkton House and its grounds, from which you may hear the cry of peacocks. You swing south-westwards, and the woodland temporarily relents to your right. Just on the edge of the next patch of woodland on the right, you will see some grassy mounds, which are in fact tumuli known as the Devil's Jumps. Shortly beyond the Devil's Jumps there is a crossroads of paths at which you turn right, as directed by a South Downs Way signpost. Follow what is an excellent track north-westwards through the woods of Philliswood Down, passing a memorial to what one assumes is a German pilot, then drop down quite steeply, swinging briefly north-eastwards then just west of north, and emerging from the trees.

You shortly arrive at a T-junction of tracks just north-east of Buriton Farm, turning left then almost immediately right onto another track. This proceeds north-westwards, and soon arrives at the corner of an area of woodland with paths forking right, into the woods, and left, round the edge. Your way is left, keeping a thickly wooded escarpment to your right, and proceeding north-westwards. You then swing slightly west of south and embark on the stiff ascent of Pen Hill, following a steep but reasonably wide track westwards. The views from the summit of Pen Hill are fantastic, and you can be forgiven a few moments to pause and enjoy them – and celebrate the fact that you are just about halfway!

Continuing westwards, you come down off Pen Hill and shortly arrive at a crossroads of paths. Ahead of you is the summit of Beacon Hill, and you could save yourself the best part of a mile by crossing straight over and scrambling up to the summit. Your route, continuing along the South Downs Way, is somewhat gentler, turning left at the crossroads and swinging firstly south-westwards then south-eastwards towards Telegraph House, ignoring a left fork. The slopes of Beacon Hill are to your right, while the ground drops steeply away to the left, with wooded slopes separating your path from Millpond Bottom. Just north of Telegraph House, not far beyond the left fork, you reach a T-junction of tracks. Turn right and now follow a good clear track round the west side of Beacon Hill, still enjoying splendid views, and descend gently to the very picturesque dry valley known as Bramshott Bottom; the slopes of Beacon Hill to your right make a particularly formidable sight.

Arriving at the head of the valley, you are now signposted south-westwards, climbing on to Harting Down. There are two parallel paths available, and you should keep to the upper path. Once you have gained the upper slopes of Harting Down you can enjoy some really lovely views to the Weald and in particular the village of South Harting with its very prominent church spire. As you come within sight of the very popular Harting Hill car park, following the upper path, you come up to a gate. Immediately before the gate you turn left, leaving the South Downs Way to follow a grassy path south-eastwards.

South Harting offers a good regular bus service back to Chichester from Monday to Saturday, and is the last practical opportunity to replenish supplies. However, when you find that to get there involves continuing along the South Downs Way past the car park to the road, turning right on to the road and following it for a mile steeply downhill with no pavement for most of the way, you may regret not popping that extra pack of Scotch eggs and bar of chocolate into your shopping basket in the Co-op last night.

Continuing away from the South Downs Way on the grassy path, you aim just to the left of an area of woodland and proceed through a large open field keeping the woods to your right. The path aims for the right-hand corner of the field – ignore paths leading into the wood to the right – and arrives at a kissing gate. Pass through the gate, and, ignoring the path leading hard right from it, bear more gently right to follow a wide track heading just east of south. Shortly you reach a crossroads of paths. Turn right and follow the track towards the road, but having passed through another kissing gate, don't go forward to the road; instead, turn left beyond the kissing gate along a path that goes parallel with the road, eventually arriving at the road itself. Cross over the road and turn left along a signed path running parallel with the road on its west side, arriving at a T-junction with a drive. Turn right onto the drive, shortly arriving at a fork; the right-hand drive leads to a private house, while you take the left-hand path.

The path, initially heading south-westwards, swings southwards, with an area of woodland to your right. Soon a public bridleway forks off to the right, but you continue in a southerly direction along the left-hand edge of open fields, with woodland to the left. The path kinks slightly to the left and meets a crossroads of paths, but you continue southwards, keeping a narrowish strip of woodland to your left, and arrive at a point where a metalled road heading east-west meets a road heading off south. You are now heading for Up Marden, which is easily reachable by following the road leading south, but the official route of the Challenge Walk turns right down the road heading west. In a few hundred yards there is a signed path leading off to the left and heading just east of south. You follow this path, ignoring black arrows pointing you hard left at the beginning. There is quite a stiff climb up a grassy incline onto the picturesquely-named Apple Down; when saying that name you can almost taste the plump, juicy fruit or refreshing tangy cider from a welcoming nearby farm shop. No such luck, sorry ...

Having gained the hilltop, go straight on across a stile and then over a crossroads of paths. You now proceed through a field, the path clearly defined, and enjoy what, on a clear day, will be tremendous views which stretch to the Isle of Wight. Ignoring a path going off to the left, continue on the main path, now heading just west of south, with some thick vegetation on the left-hand side. You arrive at a T-junction of paths and turn left onto a track which takes you to the Up Marden road. Turn right and follow the road through Up Marden. It is a pretty village with an outstandingly attractive and unfussy thirteenth-century church, which is well worth seeing if you have sufficient time and energy. Early Gothic in origin, its brick floor, simple box pews and wooden benches are, to quote Simon Jenkins, 'a study in tranquillity [...] on a summer evening we can imagine ancient peasants climbing from the fields below to find comfort and hope of salvation in their place of holiness'. The church is to be found to the right of the road, reachable from the village centre by a public footpath which is signed (the path itself, not the church).

Very shortly beyond that footpath, still in the village centre, take a signed path leading off to the left, south-eastwards. The start of it is marked by a rather unnecessary stile! The path continues somewhat unpromisingly, through a private-looking gravelly courtyard, and over two further stiles, but then enters a field. The path through the field is unclear;

you need to aim for the far *right*-hand corner of the field as you look at it, and as you approach the wood at the end of it, you will clearly see the stile giving you access to the wood. Still heading south-eastwards, you follow a clear, albeit narrow, path through the wood, and on emerging from it, swing southwards and continue forward on an obvious path through a field, going slightly downhill.

Shortly you reach a T-junction with a broader track, and you turn left to follow this track. This marks the end of rather fiddly field-path walking you have had to endure since leaving Harting Down, and you can be reassured that route-finding for the rest of the walk is much easier. This will come as pleasant news to those of you whose last reserves of mental energy drained away with the last supplies of blackcurrant Ribena in the porch of Up Marden Church.

The track proceeds confidently ahead south-eastwards, towards a large area of woodland. At the edge of the wood there is a T-junction of paths; turn left and almost immediately right to follow a track through the woods, still heading south-eastwards. This is most pleasant woodland walking, the way ahead very clear. You begin to descend, and continue quite steeply downhill, arriving at an attractive flint house on your right at the foot of the hill. At this point you reach a T-junction with the driveway serving the house; turn left onto the driveway, which is a public right of way, and arrive at a T-junction with a narrow metalled road. Turn right onto this road and follow it uphill to the point where it swings sharply right. There is a car park here and a sign for Stoughton Down, part of the delightful Kingley Vale Nature Reserve with its wealth of wildlife. You leave the road here, but by following the road on for just under a mile you reach Stoughton and its pub, which is positively the last realistic opportunity to obtain refreshment before you get back into Chichester.

The Challenge Walk, however, turns left by the sharp bend in the road and proceeds north-eastwards with woodland immediately to the right and, initially, grassland to the left. In a few hundred yards the grassland to your left gives way to woodland, and very shortly beyond this change of woodland the path swings right; ignore the left fork just here. Your path swings eastwards then south-eastwards, and it is as it turns south-eastwards that you reach a junction of forest tracks. You want the one going off to the right. There now follows a long climb through the forest, which must seem like purgatory after all the height gained – and lost – already today!

As you approach the hilltop you arrive at a big junction of paths and tracks on Stoughton Down, at which point the woodland relents to provide you with a quite superb view to the right. Continue over the junction, using the path following the same direction you have been following, that is, just east of south. Very shortly beyond, a path forks left, and you need to take this left fork. The signposting is not brilliant, but the fact is that the track going straight ahead is not a public path and could cruelly take you miles off course – ironically to an area of tumuli known as the Devil's Humps. After you have gone so far out of your way, you may feel that the Devil might not be the only one to have the hump …

Having taken the left fork, you proceed along a narrow path uphill through the woods on to Bow Hill, then begin to lose height. You pass straight over a crossroads of paths – by detouring right you will reach a quite superb hilltop viewpoint, arguably the most spectacular part of the nature reserve – then continue to descend. Emerging from the woods, you are greeted by a fantastic view of Chichester and its cathedral beckoning you home, and the surrounding coastline and countryside. You will also see once again the masts of the Trundle. Don't be complacent, though, as there is still work to do.

Having permitted yourself a pause to admire the view, descend steeply through fields to reach a crossroads of paths. You cross straight over and then, bitter irony of ironies, you must climb yet again, although the incline is much gentler than the conquest of Stoughton Down. As you climb, you proceed south-eastwards, as you've been doing since you entered the Stoughton Down woods, then having reached the crest of the hill, swing in a more easterly direction. Your hill-climbing is over!

Proceed enjoyably just south of the woodland of Stoke Clump, contouring the hillside, before shortly bending right and then right again, so you are now heading just west of south, still on the same path, gently losing height all the while. At length you reach a junction with the West Stoke–Mid Lavant road. Turn right to follow the road briefly, but almost immediately turn left onto West Stoke Road which you follow, passing the very attractive flint-built Oldwick Farm. At the end of the road you reach a crossroads; go straight over, following another minor road south-eastwards to its junction with Old Broyle Road. Turn left onto Old Broyle Road and follow it into Chichester, the surroundings becoming more and more built-up as you proceed. A convenience store on your right offers the first on-route refreshment opportunity since the Royal Oak at East Lavant!

You arrive at the very busy Northgate roundabout, all the traffic moving from right to left. Turn left to pass St Paul's Church and then cross over the busy A286, swinging right to pass the entrance to the Oaklands car park. Use the subway to pass underneath the next road, then, emerging from the subway, you then take the next left into North Street. Follow North Street all the way down to the Cross, where your pilgrimage began many, many hours ago. Your challenge walk is over. If you made it in one piece, congratulations; you can confidently approach your sponsors for their cash pledges. If you didn't, there's always the bath of baked beans.

The Beaten Track

The Big Walks of Great Britain

David Bathurst

ISBN : 1 84024 144 6
£8.99
Paperback
129 x 198 mm, 320 pages

David Bathurst laces up his walking boots as he undertakes the rough with the smooth of each of the fourteen 'big walks' of Great Britain. From a riverside amble along the Thames Path to the rigours of the Coast to Coast, this is a refreshingly humorous account of these popular and well-beaten tracks, and an appreciation of the beauty and history of the Great British countryside.

More than just a travel narrative, The Beaten Track provides detailed information on the distance, difficulties, topography and points of local interest of each walk, making it an indispensable accompaniment to any walking venture.

www.summersdale.com